EVERYDAY PR

WITH TH

EVERYDAY PRAYER BOOK

WITH THE ORDER OF MASS

Edited by

Dermot Hurley, Society of St Columban

Illustrated by the Nuns of Carisbrooke Abbey

GEOFFREY CHAPMAN

LONDON

A Geoffrey Chapman book published by
Cassell Ltd
35 Red Lion Square, London WC1R 4SG
and at Sydney, Auckland, Toronto, Johannesburg
an affiliate of Macmillan Publishing Co Inc
New York

First published 1966
Second edition 1974
Reprinted 1976
Third edition 1979
Reprinted 1980

ISBN 0 225 66273 6

Nihil obstat: R. D. Dermitius Fogarty, D.D., L.C.L.,
censor deputatus
Imprimatur: ✠ Cyrillus, Archiepiscopus Southwarcen
Datum Southwarci die 26a Junii 1965.

Printed by Fletcher & Son Ltd, Norwich

CONTENTS

INTRODUCTION

"In order that the liturgy may be able to produce its full effects, it is necessary that the faithful come to it with proper dispositions, that their minds should be attuned to their voices, and that they should co-operate with Divine Grace lest they receive it in vain . . . .

"The spiritual life, however, is not by any means limited solely to participation in the liturgy. The Christian is indeed called to pray with his brethren, but he must also enter into his chamber to pray to the Father in secret; yet more, according to the teaching of the Apostle, he should pray without ceasing" (*Constitution on the Liturgy,* Arts. 11 and 12).

The Council Fathers have reaffirmed the traditional obligation of private personal prayer, an obligation which is more ancient even than the Church herself, going back beyond the clear statements of Jesus Christ to the teaching of God in the old dispensation. As the obligation to private prayer remains, so does the necessity for prayer books, the meditation books of the laity.

This prayer book presents an abundance of prayers which have stood the test of time, so that their value is well known, many of them being prayers composed by the Fathers and saints of the Church. It is hoped that their slow and prayerful use will instill a love for prayer.

In the Community Mass section, the main prayers usually said congregationally are given in English and in Latin, which will be useful on some occasions and in some places. Prayers for the Offertory and Canon are included; it is hoped that their use will help the faithful "to be fully aware of what they are doing" (*Constitution on the Liturgy,* Art. 11) and to acquire the proper dispositions for internal participation which the Council Fathers desire. Also many prayers for Confession and Communion have been included, of such variety as to help different types of people at different times to "co-operate with divine grace", so that this important part of the liturgy "may be able to produce its full effects" (cf. *Constitution on the Liturgy,* Art. 11, quoted above).

In making new translations of some liturgical hymns, an effort was made to express the original thought closely and clearly in unrhymed verse, which in many cases may be sung to the tune of the original.

Prayers and psalms from the Old Testament, which contain some of the basic and divinely inspired expressions of man's dialogue with God, have been included in order to further the Council's injunction: "The treasures of the bible are to be opened up more lavishly, so that richer fare may be provided for the faithful at the table of God's word" (*Constitution on the Liturgy,* Art. 51). For the same reason, the Rosary, that most biblical of all popular prayers, is included, in an attempt to further appreciation of the central mystery of our redemption, by giving methods of meditating, while saying the words of the Hail Mary, on the life, death and resurrection of our Lord.

Throughout the whole book, an effort has been made to keep to simple, direct and clear language, whose meaning might be within the range even of school children, while it is hoped the matter contained is such as to satisfy any adult, no matter how advanced educationally or spiritually he may be.

Dermot Hurley
Fiji

MORNING PRAYERS

In the name of the Father, and of the Son, and of the Holy Ghost. Amen.
Blessed be the holy and undivided Trinity now and for ever. Amen.
O my God, I believe in you. Please strengthen my faith.
I hope in you. Let me trust in your love until death.
I love you with my whole heart. Teach me to love you daily more and more.
I am sorry that I have offended you. O Lord, increase my sorrow.

O my God, how good you have been to me, and how little I have done for you !
You have created me out of nothing.
You have redeemed me by the death of your Son.
You have made my soul holy by the grace of the Holy Ghost.
You have called me into your Church and you give me all the graces I need for saving my soul.
You have kept me safe during the past night,
and you have given me this new day, during which I can serve you.
How can I thank you, O Lord, for all that you have done for me ?
I will bless your holy name, and serve you all the days of my life.

MORNING OFFERING

O Jesus, through the most pure heart of Mary,
I offer you all the prayers, thoughts, works and sufferings of this day,

for all the intentions of your Sacred Heart.
I intend to gain all the indulgences I can today, for myself and the souls in purgatory.

Our Father, who art in heaven,
hallowed be thy name:
thy kingdom come:
thy will be done on earth as it is in heaven.
Give us this day our daily bread:
and forgive us our trespasses, as we forgive them who trespass against us:
and lead us not into temptation:
but deliver us from evil. Amen.

Hail Mary, full of grace,
the Lord is with thee.
Blessed art thou among women,
and blessed is the fruit of thy womb, Jesus.
Holy Mary, Mother of God,
pray for us sinners, now and at the hour of our death. Amen.

I believe in God,
the Father almighty,
creator of heaven and earth,
and in Jesus Christ, his only Son, our Lord,
who was conceived by the Holy Ghost,
born of the Virgin Mary,
suffered under Pontius Pilate,
was crucified, died and was buried;
he descended into hell;
the third day he rose again from the dead;
he ascended into heaven,
sitteth at the right hand of God the Father almighty;

from thence he shall come to judge the living and the dead.
I believe in the Holy Ghost;
the Holy Catholic Church;
the Communion of Saints;
the forgiveness of sins;
the resurrection of the body,
and life everlasting. Amen.

ACT OF FAITH

My God, I believe in you,
and in all your Church teaches,
because you have said it, and your word is true.

ACT OF HOPE

My God, I hope in you,
I am confident
that you will always give me your grace,
and bring me to heaven,
because of your promises,
your love and your power.

ACT OF LOVE

My God, I love you because you are so good.
I want to do your will in order to please you.
For your sake I love all others as myself,
and I will do all I can to help them.

ACT OF CONTRITION

O my God, I am very sorry
that I have sinned against you,
because you are so good,
and I will not sin again.

Angel of God, my guardian dear,
To whom God's love now gives me here,
Ever this day be at my side,
To light and guard, to rule and guide. Amen.

PRAYER FOR PURITY

O Mary conceived without sin,
pray for me who have recourse to you.
Hail Mary (*three times*).

MORNING HYMN (Iam Lucis Orto Sidere)

When morning's light is here again,
We come to pray to God our Lord,
That in the actions of this day,
He'll save us from our sins.

May he control and check our tongue,
Lest quarrels rise to hurt our souls,
And healing, keep our eyes from seeing
The world's tempting ways.

Let our most secret thoughts be pure,
Let foolish thoughts not waste our time,
Let abstinence of food and drink
Defeat desires of flesh.

So when the day has passed away,
And peaceful night returns again,
Let us be clean by fighting sin,
And sing our thanks to God.

To God the Father glory be,
And also to his only Son,
And Holy Ghost who comforts us,
For ever without end.

PRAYER FOR PROTECTION

Lord God almighty,
you have brought us safely to the beginning of this day.
Defend us today by your mighty power,
so that we may not fall into sin.
Protect us, so that in all our words and thoughts and actions
we may be so guided by you
as to do always what is holy in your sight. Amen.

MORNING GREETING TO GOD

My soul has desired you all night, O eternal wisdom.
And in the early morning, I turn to you with all my heart.
May your holy presence remove all dangers from my soul and body!
May your many graces fill every part of my heart
and set it on fire with your divine love.
O, most sweet Jesus, turn your face towards me,
for this morning, with all the strength of my soul,
I fly to you and salute you.
I beg of you that the thousand times thousand
angels who serve you may praise you for me,
and that the thousand times ten thousand blessed spirits who surround your throne, may glorify you for me today.
May all that is beautiful and glorious in creatures praise you for me,
May all creation bless your holy name,
which is our consoling protection in this world and for ever. Amen. (Bl. Henry Suzo O.P.)

DAILY OFFERING

Lord Jesus, I offer you my whole day;
my work, my hopes and my fight against sin,
my joys and my sorrows.
Give me and all my fellow workers the grace to think like you, to work with you, to live with you.
Make me love you with all my heart and serve you with all my strength.
May your kingdom come in all our factories,
in all our shops, in all our farms and in all our homes.
May you be better known, better loved and better served.
May those of us today who may be tempted to leave you by sin, remain in your grace. Amen.
(Adapted from a Young Christian Worker prayer.)

MORNING THANKS AND OFFERING

O sweetest Jesus, all through the dark night you have been waiting patiently
and longing for the moment when I would once more come to kneel at your blessed feet.
And now, O Jesus, I have come with my heart full of thanks to you for having spared me during the past night,
and for giving me another day to work for your greater honour and glory and for the salvation of my soul.
I offer myself entirely to you.
Make me obedient, humble and simple as a little child.
Let me be like you in love and kindness to all.
Make me resigned to your holy will.

Grant that I may be worthy of that reward which you have promised to those who love you faithfully here upon earth. Amen.

MORNING OFFERING OF ST THÉRÈSE

O my God, I offer you all my actions of this day
for the intentions and for the glory of the Sacred Heart of Jesus.
I desire to make holy every beat of my heart,
every thought of my mind,
and every single action I do,
by uniting them to its infinite merits.
I wish to get forgiveness for my sins,
and make reparation for them,
by throwing them into the fire of its merciful love.
O my God, I ask of you, for myself and for those I love,
the grace to carry out perfectly your holy will.
May we accept all the joys and sorrows of this passing life for love of you,
so that we may one day be united together in heaven for all eternity. Amen.

NIGHT PRAYERS

Our Father, who art in heaven,
hallowed be thy name:
thy kingdom come:
thy will be done on earth as it is in heaven.
Give us this day our daily bread:
and forgive us our trespasses, as we forgive them who trespass against us:
and lead us not into temptation:
but deliver us from evil. Amen.

Hail Mary, full of grace,
the Lord is with thee.
Blessed art thou among women,
and blessed is the fruit of thy womb, Jesus.
Holy Mary, Mother of God,
pray for us sinners, now and at the hour of our death. Amen.

I confess to almighty God,
to blessed Mary, ever virgin,
to blessed Michael the archangel,
to blessed John the Baptist,
to the holy apostles Peter and Paul,
and to all the saints,
that I have sinned exceedingly in thought, word, and deed,
through my fault,
through my fault,
through my most grievous fault.
Therefore I beseech the blessed Mary, ever virgin,
blessed Michael the archangel,
blessed John the Baptist,

the holy apostles Peter and Paul,
and all the saints,
to pray to the Lord our God for me.

May almighty God have mercy on me,
forgive me my sins,
and bring me to life everlasting. Amen.

May the almighty and merciful Lord
grant me pardon, absolution and remission of all my sins. Amen.

O my God, I believe that you are present here.
I believe that you see all my actions, all my thoughts, and the most secret desires of my heart.
I adore you and I love you with all my heart.
I thank you
for all the good things I have received from you, especially during this day.
Give me light, my God,
to see what sins I have committed this day,
and grant me grace to be truly sorry for them.

(Examine what you have done during the day and try to remember any sins you committed.)

ACT OF CONTRITION

O my God,
I am sorry and beg pardon for all my sins,
and detest them above all things,
because they deserve your dreadful punishments,
because they have crucified my loving Saviour Jesus Christ,
and most of all because they offend your infinite goodness;

and I firmly resolve, by the help of your grace,
never to offend you again,
and carefully to avoid the occasions of sin. Amen.

PRAYER FOR PURITY

O Mary conceived without sin,
pray for me who have recourse to you.
Hail Mary (*three times*).

In your hands, O Lord, I place my spirit;
Lord Jesus, receive my soul.

Holy Mary, be a mother to me.

May the blessed Virgin Mary,
St Joseph and all the saints
pray for me to the Lord,
that I may be preserved this night from sin and all evils. Amen.

O my good angel,
whom God has appointed to be my guardian,
watch over me during this night.
All ye angels and saints of God, pray for me.

May our Lord bless us,
and keep us from all evil,
and bring us to life everlasting;
and may the souls of the faithful departed
through the mercy of God, rest in peace. Amen.

PRAYER FOR PROTECTION

Visit, we beg of you, O Lord, this house

and drive far away from it all the temptations of the enemy.
Let your holy angels live here to keep us in peace,
and let your blessing be always upon us. Amen.

FOR A GOOD NIGHT'S REST

Bless, O Lord, the sleep I am about to take,
so that my body may be strengthened and my health increased,
that so I may be better able to serve you. Amen.

EVENING OFFERING

My dear Lord Jesus,
I offer up to you the rest I am going to take this night.
I offer it in union with that eternal rest you enjoy in the union of the Father and Holy Ghost in the blessed Trinity,
and in union with the sleep and rest you took in this world while you were living here.
I offer up to you every breath which I will draw this night,
and every movement of my heart.
I beg that they may all be so many acts
of love, praise, joy and thanksgiving to you
in union with that adoration which will be given to you in heaven,
tonight and for all eternity.
I earnestly beg that your blessed Mother,
and St Joseph,
and all the angels and saints,
may love and glorify you for me this night,
and throughout all eternity. Amen.

ACCEPTANCE OF DEATH

O my God, I accept my death,
when it will come,
as an act of honour and adoration which I owe to you, my Creator.
I accept it as a punishment due to me for my sins,
in union with the death of Jesus Christ for me on the cross,
and as the only way and means I can come to you,
my beginning and my last end. Amen.

PRAYERS FOR CONFESSION

Before Confession

O most merciful God,
I humbly thank you for all your mercies to me.
I thank you for having been so patient with me,
and for waiting so lovingly for me,
in spite of my many sins.
It is through your mercy that I have not fallen into even greater sin.
Through your love
I have been given this chance of going to confession
to seek forgiveness of all my sins.

O my God,
help me to make a good confession.
Help me to make this confession
as well as though I knew I was going to die in one hour's time.

Help me to remember my sins.
Help me to be sorry for them, and to make up my mind never to sin again.
Help me to tell them to the priest.
Strengthen my faith
so that I realise that when the priest says the words of absolution, my sins are all forgiven by you.

Holy Mary, Mother of God, pray for me that I may make a good confession.
My holy guardian angel
and all the angels and saints,
pray for me that I may make a good confession.

HELPS TO REMEMBER MY SINS

It is against God's law:

To forget the good God and my duties to him.
To say my prayers badly or not pray at all.

To use the Lord's name in a way that is wrong.
To swear without reason.
To swear something false.

On Sunday to work or miss Mass without cause.
To talk or not pray during Mass or be late.

To disobey parents or teachers or state.
To be proud, or to sulk, or to answer them back.

To give in to revenge or to anger or hate.
To get drunk or to harm others' bodies or souls.

Alone or with others to do impure acts.
Bad reading, bad talking, bad looks or bad dress.

To damage or harm what belongs to another.
To steal it or keep it, or not give it back.

To gossip. To backbite. Tell lies of excuse.
To lie about others to hurt their good name.

To consent and give in to bad thoughts or desires.
To desire others' goods. To be sad they're not mine.

Eat meat on fast Fridays, or not keep the fast.
Deliberate laziness, gluttony, pride.

Additional Prayers before Confession
(To be said if you have time.)

PRAYER FOR LIGHT

O my God,
I beg of you to grant me grace to know and hate my sins,
and grace to be truly sorry for them.

O Lord Jesus Christ,
Judge of the living and the dead,
after I die I must give to you an exact account of all my actions.
Give me light, I beg of you,
to see all the actions of my life which have offended you.
Give me humility and sorrow
that I may be able to confess them well and be really sorry for them.

Holy Mary, Mother of God, pray for me,
that I may know my sins,
that I may be truly sorry for them,
and that I may make a good confession.

PRAYER FOR GRACE TO MAKE A GOOD CONFESSION

O most loving Lord Jesus Christ,
I am not worthy to speak to you by name,
because I have so often offended you,
but receive my confession and spare me.

Do not be angry with me, O good Jesus.
Do not turn me away from your face,

because you have said that you do not desire the death of the sinner,
but that he be converted and live.

Spare me, O most kind Jesus,
who died on the cross in order to save sinners.
Have mercy on me, O most gracious Lord,
and do not refuse my humble sorrow,
because I confidently hope in your great mercy.

You have given me this desire to return to you with increased love in my soul,
and I know that you will finish this work
by giving me the grace of making a good confession.

PRAYER FOR CONTRITION

My crucified Jesus,
by your bloody sweat and agony in the garden,
by your cruel scourging at the pillar,
by your crowning with thorns,
by your three hours' agony on the cross,
by your five most precious wounds,
grant me the grace of a deep and heartfelt sorrow for my sins.

Mary, my Mother,
by all the pains that I have ever caused your loving heart,
obtain for me true sorrow for my sins.

O blessed Peter,
by the tears of sorrow you shed for denying our dear Lord,

obtain for me the grace of a deep sorrow for my sins.

O blessed Magdalen,
by the deep sorrow and burning love that filled your heart as you knelt at the feet of Jesus,
obtain for me a lasting sorrow for my sins.

O holy penitent thief,
who received the grace of sorrow and forgiveness at the last moment of your life,
as you hung on the cross beside your divine Master,
obtain for me a true and deep sorrow for my sins.

PRAYER FOR MERCY

Show me, O Lord, your mercy, and delight my heart with it.
Let me find you whom I seek with such longing.
Behold I am like the man whom the robbers seized and beat and left half dead on the road to Jericho.
Jesus Christ, kind-hearted Samaritan, come to my aid!

I am the lost sheep, wandering in the desert.
Seek after me, O good Shepherd,
bring me home again to your fold.
Do with me according to your will,
so that I may abide with you all the days of my life,
and praise you for all eternity with all those who are with you in heaven. Amen. (St Jerome.)

When you know your sins, say the "I confess" slowly, and also say a few times the act of contrition.

During your confession, remember that it is because of the death of Christ on the cross that your sins can be forgiven so easily in confession, because he has suffered the real and full punishment for your sins.

Make your confession and listen to the priest for instruction and for your penance. Say your act of contrition as though you were kneeling in front of the cross on Calvary, watching our Lord die for you and hearing his voice forgive you.

After Confession

O God the Father,
I thank you for having forgiven my sins.

O God the Son, dear Saviour,
I thank you for having died for me
and for having given me the sacrament of penance
to enable me to get rid of my sins.

O God the Holy Ghost,
I thank you for the grace you have given me of making this confession well,
and of coming with your gifts and graces into my soul.

My God,
from now on I want to love you and keep you in my soul.
Help me to love you more and more.
Help me to avoid sin in the future,
so that I may never offend you again.

I know my own weakness.
I know that if I am left to myself I will fall again soon,
but I trust in the strength of your grace and help.
Without you I can do nothing,
but with you I can do all things.
Help me always by your grace.

O Mary, my dearest Mother,
and all the angels and saints,
help me to thank God for all his graces to me,
and help me that I may never leave him again by sin.

ACT OF THANKSGIVING

I thank you, my God, for having pardoned me.
How worthy you are of my love!
May I never offend you again.
Mary, my Mother,
and all you angels and saints,
praise and thank the Lord
for his infinite goodness towards me, a poor sinner.
Amen.

ACT OF SORROW AND LOVE

O God, my Father, I have sinned before you.
I am not worthy to be called your son.
O Lord, be merciful to me, a sinner.
Have mercy on me because of your greatness,
and because of your love, forgive me my sins.

I love you, my God—even though I have sinned,
you know that I love you.

You are the God of my heart
and the God who is my choice forever.
I will always keep your law,
because it is yours, and you are my God.

PRAYER OF ST THOMAS AQUINAS FOR HOLINESS OF LIFE

O merciful God
grant that I may always do your will perfectly in all things.
May it be my desire to work only for your honour and glory.
May I rejoice in nothing except what leads to you.
May I desire nothing that leads away from you.
May all passing things be as nothing in my eyes.
May all that is yours be dear to me,
and may you, my God, be dear to me above all things.
May I desire nothing apart from you.
May all joy have no importance for me without you.
May all effort and work delight me when it is for you.

Make me O Lord
obedient without complaint,
poor without regret,
patient without murmur,
humble without pretence,
joyful without foolishness,
and truthful without disguise.

Give me, O God,
an ever watchful heart which nothing can ever draw away from you.
Give me a noble heart, which no unworthy love can ever draw down to the mire.

Give me an upright heart, which no evil can bend.
Give me an unconquerable heart which no trouble can crush.
Give me a heart full of love for you, which no bad love can claim for its own.

Give me, O God,
understanding to know you,
perseverance to seek you,
and wisdom to find you.
Give me a life which will please you,
and a hope which will unite me to you when I die. Amen.

ST GERTRUDE'S ACT OF RESOLUTION

O almighty and most merciful God,
according to your most tender mercy you have received me back once more,
after so many times that I have gone astray from you.
I give you thanks with all the strength of my soul
for this and all other mercies, graces and blessings given to me.
I throw myself down at your sacred feet,
and I offer myself to you to be yours for ever more.

Let nothing in life or death ever separate me from you;
I am sorry for all the sins of my past life.
I promise again what was promised in my baptism.

From this moment, I give myself wholly to your love and service.

Grant that for the time to come I may hate sin more than death itself,
and avoid all such occasions and company which have led me unhappily into sin.

I promise to do this with the help of your divine grace,
without which I can do nothing.
I beg your blessing on these my resolutions, O Lord,
for without you I am nothing but misery and sin.

SHORT EJACULATORY PRAYERS

Wash me fully from all my sins, O sweetest Jesus, that I may be worthy to live in your heart all the days of my life.
(St Bonaventure.)

O Heart of Jesus,
I place all my trust in you.
Though I fear all things from my weakness,
I hope all things from your mercy.
Sacred Heart of Jesus, I believe in your love for me.

Sweetest Jesus, hide me in your Sacred Heart.
Do not permit me ever to be separated from you.
Defend me from the temptations of the devil.

Lord Jesus Christ, deliver me from all my sins, and from every evil.
Make me keep your commandments
and never allow me to be separated from you.

Let you, O Lord, in your mercy,
make up for whatever faults there have been in this confession,
and give me grace to be truly sorry for my sins,
both now and always,
through Jesus Christ, your Son. Amen.

HYMNS IN HONOUR OF THE BLESSED SACRAMENT

1

O bread of heaven, beneath this veil
Thou dost my very God conceal:
My Jesus, dearest treasure, hail;
I love thee and adoring kneel;
Each loving soul by thee is fed
With thy own self in form of bread.

O food of life, thou who dost give
The pledge of immortality;
I live; no, 'tis not I that I live;
God gives me life, God lives in me:
He feeds my soul, he guides my ways,
And every grief with joy repays.

O bond of love, that dost unite
The servant to his living Lord;
Could I dare live, and not requite
Such love,—then death were meet reward:
I cannot live unless to prove
Some love for such unmeasured love.

Beloved Lord in heaven above,
There, Jesus, thou awaitest me;
To gaze on thee with changeless love;
Yes, thus, I hope, thus shall it be:
For how can he deny me heaven
Who here on earth himself hath given?

(St Alphonsus Liguori 1696–1787
Translated by E. Vaughan 1827–1908)

2

Soul of my Saviour, sanctify my breast;
Body of Christ, be thou my saving guest;
Blood of my Saviour, bathe me in thy tide,
Wash me with water flowing from thy side.

Strength and protection may thy passion be;
O blessed Jesus, hear and answer me;
Deep in thy wounds, Lord, hide and shelter me;
So shall I never, never part from thee.

Guard and defend me from the foe malign;
In death's dread moments make me only thine;
Call me, and bid me come to thee on high,
When I may praise thee with thy saints for aye.

(Attributed to Pope John XXII 1249–1334
Translator anonymous)

3

O food of travellers, angels' bread,
Manna wherewith the blest are fed,
Come nigh and with thy sweetness fill
The hungry hearts that seek thee still.

O fount of love, O well unpriced,
Outpouring from the heart of Christ,
Give us to drink of very thee,
And all we pray shall answered be.

O Jesus Christ, we pray to thee
That this thy presence which we see,
Though now in form of bread concealed.
To us may be in heaven revealed.

(Maintzisch Gesangbuch 1661
Translated by Walter H. Shewring and others)

4

Of the glorious body telling,
O, my tongue, its mysteries sing,
And the blood, all price excelling,
Which the world's eternal king,
In a noble womb once dwelling,
Shed for this world's ransoming.

Given for us, for us descending,
Of a virgin to proceed,
Man with man in converse blending,
Scattered he the gospel seed,
Till his sojourn drew to ending,
Which he closed in wondrous deed.

At the last great supper lying
Circled by his brethren's band,
Meekly with the law complying,
First he finished its command,
Then, immortal food supplying,
Gave himself with his own hand.

Word made flesh, by word he maketh
Very bread his flesh to be;
Man in wine Christ's blood partaketh:
And if senses fail to see,
Faith alone the true heart waketh
To behold the mystery.

This hymn is continued under No 5

5
Therefore we, before him bending,
This great sacrament revere;
Types and shadows have their ending,
For the newer rite is here;
Faith, our outward sense befriending,
Makes the inward vision clear.

Glory let us give, and blessing
To the Father, and the Son;
Honour, might, and praise addressing,
While eternal ages run;
Ever too his love confessing,
Who, from both, with both is one.

(St Thomas Aquinas 1227–74
Translated by J. M. Neale 1818–66,
E. Caswall 1814–78, and others)

STATIONS OF THE CROSS

In addition to the special prayers which follow, say also the following prayer at each station, if you have time:

My God, I love you
with my whole heart and above all things
and am heartily sorry that I have offended you.
May I never offend you any more.
Oh, may I love you without ceasing,
and make it my delight to do in all things your
most holy will.

1st Station

JESUS IS CONDEMNED TO DEATH

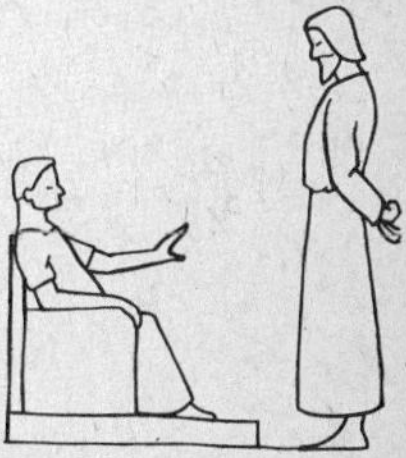

My Jesus, you received that sentence of death silently and gladly for love of me. When I am unkindly or unjustly treated, help me to bear it patiently and silently for love of you, dear Lord.

2nd Station

THE CROSS IS LAID ON THE SHOULDERS OF JESUS

Dear Jesus, you welcomed and carried the cross on your bleeding shoulders for love of me. O, grant that I also may accept my sorrows lovingly for you, O Lord.

3rd Station

JESUS FALLS THE FIRST TIME UNDER THE CROSS

My Jesus, you fell under the heavy weight of the cross that you carried to make up for my sins. O grant, dear Lord, that through the merits of that first fall, I may never fall into sin.

4th Station

JESUS MEETS HIS SORROWFUL MOTHER

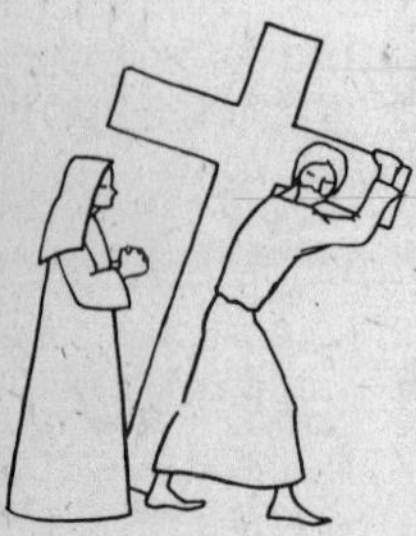

O Jesus, what pain you suffered when you met your mother on the way to Calvary!
O Mary, what heartbreaking suffering it was for you to see your dear Son carrying that heavy cross on his shoulders! Mother of sorrows, obtain for me a great love for Jesus, and a great sorrow for my sins which caused his sufferings. O dear Jesus, give me a great love for your own dear Mother.

5th Station

SIMON OF CYRENE HELPS JESUS TO CARRY HIS CROSS

O Jesus, I would have loved to help you carry your cross. O help me to bear my own sufferings patiently for love of you. Make me remember that when I help others, I am helping you.

6th Station

VERONICA WIPES THE FACE OF JESUS

My Jesus, St Veronica wiped the sweat and blood from your suffering face. You were pleased by her kindness, and left the imprint of your holy face on her towel. Help me to remember that I can show my love for you by being kind to those around me.

7th Station

JESUS FALLS THE SECOND TIME

My Jesus, you fell again under the weight of your heavy cross, but had to get up and continue your painful journey. Grant that I may never fall into mortal sin, but if I do, grant that I may rise up quickly and love you again.

8th Station

JESUS COMFORTS THE WOMEN OF JERUSALEM

My Jesus, when some women in the crowd had pity on you and wept for you, you forgot your own sufferings, and comforted them. Help and comfort me also. Give me the grace never to pity myself in my troubles, but to forget myself and my sorrows when others need my help and pity.

9th Station

JESUS FALLS THE THIRD TIME

Jesus when you fell for the third time, it was harder than ever before to drag your tired and suffering body up from the ground and to continue your journey to Calvary. Grant me the grace to rise up from all my sins and leave them behind me, even though it may sometimes be difficult for me.

10th Station

JESUS IS STRIPPED OF HIS CLOTHES

My Jesus, the cruel soldiers tore off your clothes and the wounds of your body started bleeding again. Oh, my suffering Jesus, I love you with all my heart. Strip me of all love for everything which offends you.

11th Station

JESUS IS NAILED TO THE CROSS

My Jesus, you felt the sharp pain when the nails were driven into your hands and feet. It was my sins which caused you this pain. O grant that I may never offend you again by even one deliberate sin. Grant that I may be able to accept my sufferings patiently by remembering your sufferings for me.

12th Station

JESUS DIES ON THE CROSS

My Jesus, when your enemies raised up the cross, you hung in pain for three hours and then died for me, to redeem me and give me the chance of going to heaven. O dear Lord, grant that I may live and die for love of you. Grant that I may be always faithful to your sacraments which you gave to your Church and which bring the grace of Calvary to my soul.

Holy Mary, when you watched your Son dying on the cross, your heart was breaking because of his sufferings and because you were not able to help him. He gave us to you as your children. Help us and watch over us. Take care of us and bring us to Jesus when we die.

13th Station

JESUS IS LAID IN THE ARMS OF HIS SORROWING MOTHER

O Mother of Sorrows, you suffered great agony when you received the dead body of your Son into your arms, and when you remembered all that happened during your happy life together with him in Bethlehem and Nazareth. O Mother, obtain for me a great love for Jesus, and a great sorrow and hatred of sin, so that I may never again offend him.

14th Station

JESUS IS PLACED IN THE TOMB

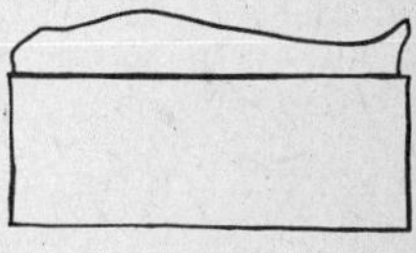

My Jesus, three days after your weeping mother and friends placed you in your tomb, you rose again, and gave back to them a joy that never left them. Help me not to be afraid of death. Help me to remember the life of happiness you desire me to enjoy after death. Strengthen my faith and the faith of all my friends when we have to watch the burials of our dearest friends, and comfort us in our sorrows.

JESUS

THE JESUS PSALTER

The following prayers are repeated after each of the fifteen petitions:

Have mercy on all sinners, Jesus, I beg of you.
Turn their vices into virtues.
Make them true followers of your law.
Bring them to happiness in everlasting glory.

Have mercy also on the souls in purgatory,
I beg of you,
because of your bitter passion,
and for your glorious name's sake, O Jesus.

O Blessed Trinity, One Eternal God, have mercy on me.
Our Father . . . Hail Mary . . .

The following prayer may be said at the end of each group of petitions:

Our Lord Jesus Christ humbled himself and
became obedient to death,
even to the death of the cross.

Hear these my petitions,
O my most merciful Saviour.
Grant me grace to repeat and consider them often,
so that they may help my soul to increase in
knowing, loving and serving you and my
neighbour,
throughout my whole life. Amen.

FIRST PETITION

Jesus, Jesus, Jesus, have mercy on me

(Say slowly three times)

Jesus, have mercy on me, and forgive the many and great sins which I have committed against you.

I have often been senseless in my life, and I have deserved great sufferings for my ingratitude.

Have mercy on me, dear Jesus, for I am weak;
O Lord, help me, for I am unable to help myself.

Keep me from giving my heart to any of your creatures, in such a way as to turn away my eyes from always looking up to you.

Grant me the grace from now on to hate sin, for love of you; and to despise all the foolish things of this world, because of my true love for you.

Have mercy on all sinners . . .

SECOND PETITION

Jesus, Jesus, Jesus, help me

(Say slowly three times)

Jesus help me to overcome all temptations to sin and to be strong against the hatred of my spiritual enemy, the devil.

Help me to spend my time in holy actions, and in doing such work as you wish me to do.

Help me to fight against and defeat the temptations of my body to laziness, gluttony and impurity.

Help my soul to love holiness, and to burn with desire to be united to you.

Help me to deserve and keep my good name by peaceful and holy living, for your honour, O Jesus, for my own happiness and for the benefit of others.

Have mercy on all sinners . . .

THIRD PETITION

Jesus, Jesus, Jesus, strengthen me

(Say slowly three times)

Jesus strengthen me in soul and body, so that I may please you by doing the works of holiness that will bring me your everlasting joy and happiness.

Grant me a firm intention, most merciful Saviour, to change my sinful life. Help me to make reparation for the past years, because I have spent many of them badly, displeasing you by sinful thoughts, words, deeds and bad habits.

Make my heart obedient to your will. Make it ready for your love, and ready to perform all the works of mercy which I can.

Grant me the gifts of the Holy Ghost, which may bring me to your heavenly kingdom, by helping me to live a good life and to receive your sacraments often.

Have mercy on all sinners . . .

FOURTH PETITION

Jesus, Jesus, Jesus, comfort me

(Say slowly three times)

Jesus comfort me, and give me grace to look for my joy and happiness in you alone.

Fill me with thoughts of heaven, with spiritual sweetness and loving desires for your glory. Fill my soul with the remembrance of heaven, where I hope to live for ever with you.

Remind me often of your infinite goodness, of your gifts and of the great kindness you have shown to me.

And when you remind me of my sins, comfort me with the certainty of obtaining your grace by a perfect spirit of sorrow, which will take away my guilt and prepare me for your kingdom.

Have mercy on all sinners . . .

FIFTH PETITION

Jesus, Jesus, Jesus, make me constant

(Say slowly three times)

Jesus, make me constant in faith, hope and charity. Give me perseverance in all the virtues, and resolution never to offend you.

May the memory of your passion and of the bitter pains which you suffered for me, strengthen my patience, and comfort me in all troubles and trials.

May I always hold fast to the teachings of your Catholic Church, and may I always practise the duties of my religion.

May no false delight of this deceitful world blind me. May no temptation of my body or of the devil shake my heart from its love for you; for my heart aims to rest in you forever, and to remember that nothing is of more value than heaven.

Have mercy on all sinners . . .

SIXTH PETITION

Jesus, Jesus, Jesus, enlighten me with spiritual wisdom

(Say slowly three times)

Jesus, enlighten me with spiritual wisdom to know your goodness and all those things which are most pleasing to you.

Help me to realise clearly that my only good is to love you, and give me strength always to arrange my life according to your holy will.

Grant that I may wisely proceed from virtue to virtue, till at last I reach heaven and see your glorious majesty face to face.

Do not permit me, dear Lord, to return to those sins for which I have been sorry, and which have been forgiven by contrition and confession.

Grant me grace to help the souls of others by my good advice, and to win back those who turn against you.

Have mercy on all sinners . . .

SEVENTH PETITION

Jesus, Jesus, Jesus, grant me the grace to fear you

(Say slowly three times)

Jesus, grant me grace to fear you and to avoid all occasions of offending you.

May your warnings of the punishment of sinners, and the fear of losing your love and your heavenly kingdom, always keep me from sin.

May I be afraid to remain in the state of sin, but soon return to repentance, lest the terrible sentence of endless death and damnation fall upon me.

May the powerful prayers of your blessed Mother and your saints and above all your own merits and mercy, O my Saviour, always protect my poor soul from your punishing justice.

May I be able, O my God, to work out my salvation with fear and trembling; and may the fear of your secret judgments cause me always to seek your grace carefully and humbly.

Have mercy on all sinners . . .

EIGHTH PETITION

Jesus, Jesus, Jesus, grant me grace to love you

(Say slowly three times)

Jesus, grant me grace truly to love you because of your infinite goodness, and because of the wonderful gifts which I have received in the past from you.

May the remembrance of your kindness and patience conquer the badness and sinful weakness of my stubborn nature.

May the thought of the many times you have forgiven me and of the many graces and helps you have given to me make me ashamed of not thanking and loving you.

In return for all your mercies, all you want from me is that I love you.

You desire my love, because you are my only good.

O my dear Lord, my whole life will be a desire for you. Because I do indeed love you, I will most carefully keep your commandments, which your love has given me for my benefit.

Have mercy on all sinners . . .

NINTH PETITION

Jesus, Jesus, Jesus, grant me grace to remember my death

(Say slowly three times)

Jesus, grant me grace always to remember my death, and the great judgment which will follow, so that my soul may be always in the state of grace, and may leave this life in your love.

When my death comes, deliver me by the holy prayers of your blessed Mother, and the help of the glorious St Michael, from the enemy of my soul. My good angel, help me in that most important hour.

In that day, remember your mercy, dear Jesus, and turn not your most loving face away from me because of my sins.

Make me safe against the terrors of that day, by causing me now to die each day to all earthly things, so that my thoughts and my love may always be directed towards heaven.

May the remembrance of your death teach me how

to value my life. May the memory of your resurrection encourage me to die cheerfully.

Have mercy on all sinners . . .

TENTH PETITION

Jesus, Jesus, Jesus, send me here my purgatory

(Say slowly three times)

Jesus, send me here my purgatory, and so save me from the pains of that cleansing fire, which in the next world awaits those souls who have not been sufficiently cleansed from sin in this world.

Send me those merciful crosses and sufferings, which you know are necessary to keep me from loving the things of this world too much.

No one who loves any other thing more than you can see you in heaven. Therefore, do not allow my heart to find rest in anything here, except in you alone.

After death, the suffering of a soul that is separated from you will be bitter, because it desires to come to you but is prevented by the heavy chains of sin.

Therefore, my Saviour, in this life keep me continually mortified to the world, so that, being completely purified by the fire of your love, I may immediately pass when I die into the possession of your eternal kingdom.

Have mercy on all sinners . . .

ELEVENTH PETITION

Jesus, Jesus, Jesus, grant me the grace to avoid bad company

(Say slowly three times)

Jesus, grant me the grace to avoid bad company. If I chance to fall in with any bad companions, I beg of you by the merits of your most pure conversation among sinners, to save me from being overcome by any temptation to sin.

Let me always remember with fear that you always hear and see me, and that you will take an account of all my words and actions and will judge me accordingly when I die.

May I never seek the company of slanderers, liars, drunkards or swearers. May I always keep away from those whose conversation is either quarrelsome, impure or vain.

Overcome in me, dear Jesus, all sinful love of bodily pleasure, and of the delight of taste. Grant me grace to avoid such company as would strengthen these unruly desires.

May your power defend me. May your wisdom guide me. May your fatherly pity punish me. Make me so to live in this world among men, that I may be fit for the company of angels hereafter in heaven.

Have mercy on all sinners . . .

TWELFTH PETITION

Jesus, Jesus, Jesus, grant me the grace to call on you for help

(Say slowly three times)

Jesus, grant me grace in all my needs to call on you for help, faithfully remembering your death and resurrection for me.

Do not be deaf to my cries, you who were pleased to lay down your life for my salvation. I know you are able to save me now, you who were able to take up your life again in order to lead me to my reward.

You are my best and truest friend in heaven. O my Jesus, I am full of joy when I remember your words, "Come to me all you who labour and are heavily burdened, and I will refresh you."

You are my sure defence against every kind of enemy. You are my help, ready to strengthen me in every good work.

Therefore in all my sufferings, weaknesses and temptations, I will confidently call on you, O my Jesus, and when you hear my call, have mercy on me.

Have mercy on all sinners . . .

THIRTEENTH PETITION

Jesus, Jesus, Jesus, make me persevere in virtue

(Say slowly three times)

Jesus, make me persevere in virtue and in a good life. Never allow me to stop serving you, until you bring me to my reward in your kingdom.

Continue to strengthen, O Lord, my soul and body in my religious exercises, in the duties of my religion, and in all my honest and necessary work.

Our life is a journey on earth towards our home in heaven, which he that sits down or turns aside can never reach.

O Jesus, make me always consider your blessed example: through much pain and with little pleasure, you pressed on to a bitter death, which was the way to a glorious resurrection.

Make me, O Redeemer, give serious thought to those words of yours, "He that perseveres to the end shall be saved."

Have mercy on all sinners . . .

FOURTEENTH PETITION

Jesus, Jesus, Jesus, grant me grace to fix my mind on you

(Say slowly three times)

Jesus, grant me grace to fix my mind on you, especially in the time of prayer, when I talk directly to you.

Stop the movements of my wandering mind and the desires of my restless heart. Overcome the power of my spiritual enemies, who at the time of prayer try to draw my mind from heavenly thoughts to many vain distractions.

Let me remember with joy and gratitude that it is you who have delivered me from all the evils I have escaped, you who have given me all the good I have ever received.

May I remember that you are my only good and that you intend all other things only as helps to fix my mind on you. Make me love you more and more, and by my loving you, make me happy for all eternity.

O beloved of my soul, guide all my thoughts here, so that my eyes, keeping away from all foolish and harmful sights, may become worthy to see you face to face in your glory for ever.

Have mercy on all sinners . . .

FIFTEENTH PETITION

Jesus, Jesus, Jesus, give me grace to direct my life towards my eternal welfare

(Say slowly three times)

Jesus, give me grace to direct my life towards my eternal welfare, with love and wisdom offering all the actions of my body and soul to obtain the reward of your eternal happiness.

For this world is a school to raise up souls and make them fit for the other world. And how are they made fit, except by an eager desire to enjoy God, their only end?

Break my stubborn spirit, O Jesus, and make it humble and obedient. Grant me grace to leave this life with contempt for the world, and with a heart full of joy because I am going to you.

May the memory of your passion make me cheerfully bear all temptations and sufferings here for love of you. May my soul desire that happy life and unending glory which you have prepared in heaven for your servants.

O Jesus, let me often and carefully remember that, no matter what I gain, all is lost if I lose you: and that no matter what I lose, all is gained, if I gain you.

Have mercy on all sinners . . .

PRAYERS FROM THE OLD TESTAMENT

PRAYER FOR MERCY AND FORGIVENESS

You are just, O Lord,
and all your judgments are just,
and all your ways
are mercy and truth and judgment.

And now, O Lord, think of me,
and take not revenge of my sins,
neither remember my offences
nor those of my parents.

For we have not obeyed your commandments;
therefore are we delivered
to captivity and death.

O Lord, do with me according to your will,
and command my spirit
to be received in peace;
for it is better for me to die than to live.

You are great, O Lord, for ever,
and your kingdom is unto all ages.

For you scourge, and you save;
you lead down to hell, and bring up again,
and there is none that can escape your hand.
(From Tobias 32.)

PRAYER AGAINST TEMPTATION

O Lord, Father and sovereign ruler of my life,
leave me not to the temptations of my enemies,
nor suffer me to fall by them.
Who will set scourges over my thoughts,
and the discipline of wisdom over my heart,
lest my ignorance increase,
and my offences be multiplied,
and my sins abound,
and my enemy rejoice over me?
O Lord, Father and God of my life,
leave me not to their snares.
Give me not pride of my eyes,
and turn away from me all coveting.
Take from me the greediness of the belly,
and let not the lusts of the flesh take hold of me,
and give me not over
to a shameless and foolish mind.
(From Ecclesiasticus 23.)

PRAYER FOR MERCY

Hear, O Lord, and have mercy
for you are a merciful God,
Have pity on us,
for we have sinned before you.
You remain for ever,
and shall we perish everlastingly?
O Lord almighty, the God of Israel,
think upon your hand
and upon your name at this time;
For you are the Lord, our God
and we shall praise you, O Lord.
(From Baruch 3.)

PRAYER THAT GOD MAY BE GLORIFIED

Have mercy on us, O God of all.
And behold us, and send us
the light of your mercies.

And send your fear upon the nations
that have not sought after you:
That they may know
that there is no God beside you,
and that they may show forth your wonders.

Lift up your hand over the strange nations,
that they may see your power.
For as you have been sanctified
in us in their sight
so you shall be praised
among them in our presence:
That they may know you,
as we also have known you,
that there is no God beside you, O Lord.

Renew your signs and work new miracles,
Glorify your hand and your right arm.

Hasten the time and remember the end,
that they may declare your wonderful works.

Have mercy on your people
upon whom your name is called,

Reward them that patiently await you,
and hear the prayers of your servants.

(From Ecclesiasticus 36.)

PRAYER IN PRAISE OF GOD'S MERCY

I will give glory to you,
O Lord my king,
And I will praise you,
O God my Saviour.
I will give glory to your name,
for you have been a helper and protector to me,
And have preserved my body from destruction,
from the snare of an unjust tongue,
and from the lips of them that forge lies,
And in the sight of them that stood by
you have been my helper.
My soul shall praise the Lord,
even unto death.
They surrounded me on every side,
and there was no one that would help me.
I looked for the help of men,
and there was none.
I remembered your mercy, O Lord, and your works
which are from the beginning of the world.
How you deliver them that wait for you, O Lord.
I called upon the Lord,
that he would not leave me in the day of my trouble,
and in the time of pride without help.
And my prayer was heard.
Therefore I will give thanks and praise you,
and bless the name of the Lord.
(From Ecclesiasticus 51.)

PRAYER OF THANKSGIVING AND PRAISE

I will give thanks to you, O Lord,
for you were angry with me.
Your wrath is turned away:

and you have comforted me.
Behold God is my Saviour:
I will work confidently and will not fear,
Because the Lord is my strength and my praise,
and he is become my salvation.
Praise ye the Lord,
and call upon his name.
Make his works known among the people,
remember that his name is high.
Sing ye to the Lord,
for he has done great things;
show this forth in all the earth.
(From Isaiah 12.)

PRAYER OF PRAISE AND PETITION

O Lord, Lord, almighty King,
all things are in your power,
and there is none that can resist your will.
You have made heaven and earth,
and all things
that are under the shelter of the sky.
And now, O Lord, O King, O God of Abraham,
have mercy on your people,
because our enemies resolve to destroy us,
and to wipe out your inheritance.
Hear my prayers, and
turn my mourning into joy,
that we may live and praise your name, O Lord.
(From Esther 13.)

PRAYER OF CONFIDENCE AND LOVE

O Lord, you are my God,
I will exalt you

and give glory to your name,
for you have done wonderful things.
Because you have been a strength to the poor,
a strength to the needy in his distress.
This is our God,
we have waited for him,
and he will save us.
This is the Lord,
we have patiently waited for him,
we shall rejoice
and be joyful in his salvation.
O Lord,
we have patiently waited for you,
Your name and your remembrance
are the desire of my soul.
My soul has desired you in the night
and in the morning early
I will watch for you.
Lord, you will give us peace,
for you have arranged all our works for us.
O Lord, our God, only in you
let us remember your name.
(From Isaiah 25.)

PRAYER OF CONFIDENCE

O Lord the hope of Israel,
all that forsake you
shall be confounded;
they that shall depart from you
shall be beaten to the earth
because they have forsaken the Lord,
the source of living waters.
Heal me, O Lord, and I shall be healed,

Save me and I shall be saved,
for you are my praise.
And I am not troubled,
following you for my shepherd.
And you know
I have not desired the disaster of man.
Do not be a terror unto me.
You are my hope
in the day of affliction.
Let them be confounded that persecute me,
and let me not be confounded.
Let them be afraid,
and let me not be afraid.
(From Jeremiah 17.)

PRAYER OF PRAISE AND LOVE

You have ordered all things
in measure and number and weight.
Great power always belongs to you alone,
and who shall resist the strength of your arm?
For the whole world before you
is as the least grain of the balance,
and as drop of the morning dew
that falls down upon the earth.
But you have mercy on all,
because you can do all things,
and you overlook the sins of men
for the sake of repentance.
For you love all things that are,
and hate none of the things
which you have made:
for you did not appoint or make anything,
hating it.

And how could anything endure,
if you willed it not,
or be preserved,
if not called by you?
But you spare all,
because they are yours,
O Lord who love souls.
How good and sweet is your spirit O Lord,
in all things!
For there is no other God but you,
who have care of all
that you should show
that you do not give judgment unjustly.
(From Wisdom II.)

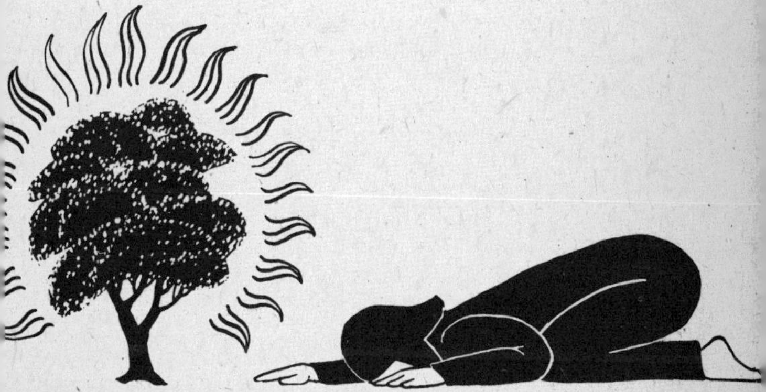

PRAYERS TO THE HOLY GHOST

COME HOLY GHOST

VENI CREATOR SPIRITUS

Come, Holy Ghost, who made all things;
Come to the souis you made your own;
Come fill with all your heavenly grace
The hearts that you created here.

Come! You are called our Advocate,
The most high God's great gift to us.
Come, living source of burning love,
To heal our souls and give them rest.

Come bring to us your seven gifts;
God works through you his holy will.
He promised you and sent you here,
To help us always say what's right.

Come, give us light to guide our lives;
Come, pour your love into our hearts;
Come, make our weakened bodies strong
With your almighty strength and grace.

Come, drive away our enemy
And give instead your own true peace.
With you, our leader, showing the way,
We'll leave behind all hurtful sin.

To know the Father, teach us now;
May we through you know Jesus too.
May we believe in you always—
The Father's Spirit and the Son's.

To God the Father glory be,
And to the Son who rose again,
And also to the Holy Ghost,
While everlasting ages pass.

COME TO US, O HOLY GHOST

VENI SANCTE SPIRITUS

Come to us, O Holy Ghost;
Bring us heaven's light and grace;
Guide our actions here on earth.

Come, dear lover of the poor;
Come, sweet giver of good gifts;
Come, give light to human hearts.

Come, consoler best of all,
Come to live within our souls;
Come, renew our strength and joy.

When we're weak from effort bring ease;
Bring cool rest from passion's heat;
Come to change our tears to joy.

Come, most blessed light of God;
Come to fill the hearts and minds
Of your faithful people here.

If we lose your grace and help,
We have nothing left that's good,
All our lives will turn to sin.

Come to wash away our faults;
Come to make our virtues strong;
Come to heal the wounds of sin.

Soften souls now hard through sin;
Give warm life to love grown cold;
Guide the lives that turn from God.

Come to give your faithful ones,
Come to give your trusting ones
All your seven mighty gifts.

Come reward our lives at death;
Help us then to save our souls;
Give the joy that never ends.

PRAYER FOR LIGHT

May your brightness shine on us, almighty God,
and may the Holy Spirit,
the light of your light,
enlighten and strengthen the hearts of all of us,
who are made new by your grace.
(Collect for Eve of Pentecost.)

Come, Holy Spirit, fill the hearts of your faithful
enkindle in them the fire of your divine love.
Send forth your Spirit,
and make new the face of the earth.

PRAYERS FOR THE SICK AND DYING

FOR THE SICK

O Lord Jesus, when you were on earth you had pity on the sick and cured their diseases. Hear our prayer now, as we ask you to give your merciful help to . . . (name the sick person) . . . who is sick. Give him back good health, so that he may live to praise you and to serve you.

FOR A SICK CHILD

Under your hand, O God, all things grow and grown things are strengthened. Stretch out your hand over this child of yours, who is young and sick, so that he (or she) may be restored to health and live a long life, your true and grateful servant throughout his whole life. Through our Lord Jesus Christ. Amen.
(From *The Layman's Missal.*)

AT THE ANOINTING OF THE SICK

Lord God, you said through your apostle James: "Is one of you sick? Then let him send for the ministers of the Church, and let them pray over him, anointing him with oil in the Lord's name. Prayer offered in faith will restore the sick man, and the Lord will give him relief; if he is guilty of sins, they will be pardoned."
Therefore we beg you, O God our Redeemer, by the grace of the Holy Spirit, heal this sick person of his illness. Cure his sickness; forgive his sins; take

away from him all pain of mind and body. Have mercy on him, and restore him to full health in body and soul so that, made whole by your goodness, he may again go about his daily life and work: you who live and reign with the Father and the Holy Spirit, one God, for ever and ever. Amen.

Look, Lord, on your servant in his weakness and weariness, and strengthen the soul you have created, so that suffering may make him holy, and he may grow better through your health-giving sacrament. Through our Lord Jesus Christ. Amen.

(From *The Layman's Missal*.)

FOR THE DYING

Go forth, O Christian soul,
out of this world,
in the name of God the Father almighty,
who created you;
in the name of Jesus Christ, the Son of the
living God, who suffered for you;
in the name of the Holy Spirit,
who was given to you;
in the name of the holy and glorious Mary, Virgin
Mother of God;
in the name of blessed Joseph;
in the name of the angels, archangels, thrones
and dominations;
in the name of the patriarchs and prophets,
of the holy apostles and evangelists,
of the holy martyrs, confessors, monks and hermits,
of the holy virgins,
and of all the saints of God;

may peace be yours this day, and may your home be in heaven.
Through the same Christ our Lord. Amen.

God of mercy, God of pity,
again and again your mercy blots out the sins of penitent sinners,
and wipes away the stain of their sin,
Look kindly upon this servant of yours,
and forgive the wrong he has done you,
for with all his heart he admits that he has done it, and only asks for pardon.
Human weakness and the devil's snares
have done much evil in his soul.
Undo this harm,
and make him again a sound member of your Church.
Hear his sorrowful prayers, O Lord,
see his tears, and pity him.
He has no other hope except your mercy.
Show him your mercy, therefore,
and take him back to you.
Through Christ Jesus our Lord. Amen.

AT THE POINT OF DEATH

Into your hands, O Lord, I entrust my spirit.
O Lord Jesus Christ, receive my soul.
Holy Mary, pray for me.
Mary, mother of grace, mother of mercy,
defend me from the enemy;
receive me at the hour of death.
Saint Joseph, pray for me.
Saint Joseph, with your blessed Virgin Spouse,

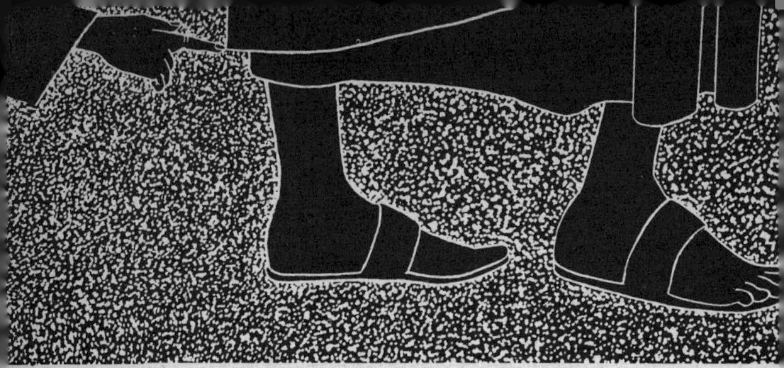

open wide for me the arms of God's mercy.
Jesus, Mary, Joseph, I give you my heart and my soul.
Jesus, Mary, Joseph, be with me and help me in my last agony.
Jesus, Mary, Joseph, may I sleep and take my rest in peace with you.
Lord have mercy,
Christ have mercy,
Lord have mercy.

IN THE PRESENCE OF THE DEAD

We commend to you, O Lord, the soul of your servant . . . (name him).
Dead to this world, may he find life with you.
In your merciful goodness
forgive the sins he has committed in this life
through human weakness.
Through Christ our Lord. Amen.

ROSARY THOUGHTS

The words of the Hail Mary were first used to praise our Lady by God himself, because the angel Gabriel was "sent by God", and Elizabeth was "filled with the Holy Ghost" when they first spoke these words to our Lady. In the Hail Mary you are using these same words in praise of our Lady and her Son.

Each decade of the Rosary brings us a new mystery or event in our Lady's life to think about, and the words of the Hail Mary will have a different meaning for us as we think of each different mystery.

Try to address your words to our Lady, as you imagine her taking part in each of these events of her life. Imagine you are there with her and say the words of the Hail Mary *to* her, and *to* her Son, Jesus Christ.

The following thoughts will give some help in doing this. It is usually enough to think of one of the little explanations or thoughts during each Hail Mary, changing from one to another as we desire.

The thoughts should not be said; nor should they be read while saying the Hail Mary. It is better to glance at them before each decade, and fix one or two in mind, and then close the eyes and try to see or imagine our Lady so as to be able to speak to her the words of the Hail Mary. You should open your eyes to pick another thought only when you find yourself becoming distracted.

When we say, "Pray for us sinners", the word ". . . us . . ." reminds us that we are not praying for ourselves alone. Remember as we use it, to unite ourselves in mind either with the particular people we are praying for or with the whole human race. We add the word ". . . sinners . . ." to confess that we, personally, have added to the sins and suffering of the world and, together with all other sinners, need God's mercy. It is *charity* never to pray for ourselves, without praying also for "... sinners ..."; it is *humility* never to pray for "... sinners ..." without including ourselves also.

THE ANNUNCIATION

Imagine that we are watching our Lady as the angel Gabriel tells her that she is to be the Mother of God, and as Christ became man in her womb for our redemption. Look at her in our minds and say to her in praise:

HAIL MARY, FULL OF GRACE,
hearing the angel giving you this wonderful news.

THE LORD IS WITH THEE,
living in your womb.

BLESSED ART THOU AMONG WOMEN,
because God has chosen you as his mother.

BLESSED IS THE FRUIT OF THY WOMB, JESUS.
becoming man in order to die for us.

HOLY MARY, MOTHER OF GOD, PRAY FOR US SINNERS, NOW, AND AT THE HOUR OF OUR DEATH. AMEN.

THE VISITATION

Imagine that we are making the journey with Mary to Elizabeth's home, and watching her meeting her cousin. Let us say to her:

HAIL MARY, FULL OF GRACE,
full of holiness and love without the slightest stain of sin.

THE LORD IS WITH THEE,
in your womb on this journey of love.

BLESSED ART THOU AMONG WOMEN,
for no one else is the Mother of God but you.

BLESSED IS THE FRUIT OF THY WOMB, JESUS.
being pleased at your charity and kindness.

HOLY MARY, MOTHER OF GOD, PRAY FOR US SINNERS, NOW, AND AT THE HOUR OF OUR DEATH. AMEN.

THE NATIVITY

Let us imagine that we are present in the stable at Bethlehem, with Mary and her Son, Jesus, who is just born. Let us say to her:

HAIL MARY, FULL OF GRACE,
lovingly looking on your newly born Son.

THE LORD IS WITH THEE,
near you in the manger, or in your arms.

BLESSED ART THOU AMONG WOMEN,
because your Son is God.

BLESSED IS THE FRUIT OF THY WOMB, JESUS.
who was born to save us.

HOLY MARY, MOTHER OF GOD, PRAY FOR US SINNERS, NOW, AND AT THE HOUR OF OUR DEATH. AMEN.

THE PRESENTATION

Let us imagine that we are watching Mary taking the Infant Jesus to the temple at Jerusalem, and offering him to God according to the Law as an act of obedience and honour to God. And let us say to her:

HAIL MARY, FULL OF GRACE,
lovingly minding Jesus on this journey.

THE LORD IS WITH THEE,
as you watch the priest offer him to God.

BLESSED ART THOU AMONG WOMEN,
because the Son whom you offer is God.

BLESSED IS THE FRUIT OF THY WOMB, JESUS.
offering his whole life and death to God.

HOLY MARY, MOTHER OF GOD, PRAY FOR US SINNERS, NOW, AND AT THE HOUR OF OUR DEATH. AMEN.

THE FINDING IN THE TEMPLE

Let us imagine that we are watching Mary as she finds Jesus after looking for him for three days. Let us rejoice with her, and say to her:

HAIL MARY, FULL OF GRACE,
happy at having found your Son.

THE LORD IS WITH THEE,
back again with you after having been lost.

BLESSED ART THOU AMONG WOMEN,
because the Son whom you found is God.

BLESSED IS THE FRUIT OF THY WOMB, JESUS.
giving joy to you when you find him.

HOLY MARY, MOTHER OF GOD, PRAY FOR US SINNERS, NOW, AND AT THE HOUR OF OUR DEATH. AMEN.

THE AGONY IN THE GARDEN

Let us imagine that we are with our Lady as she hears about the sufferings of Jesus in the garden. Let us try to comfort her and say to her:

HAIL MARY, FULL OF GRACE,
full of sorrow, too.

THE LORD IS WITH THEE,
in your mind and heart as you hear of his sufferings.

BLESSED ART THOU AMONG WOMEN,
because you willingly allowed Jesus to suffer for us.

BLESSED IS THE FRUIT OF THY WOMB, JESUS.
remembering our sins, yet glad to die for us.

HOLY MARY, MOTHER OF GOD, PRAY FOR US SINNERS, NOW, AND AT THE HOUR OF OUR DEATH. AMEN.

THE SCOURGING AT THE PILLAR

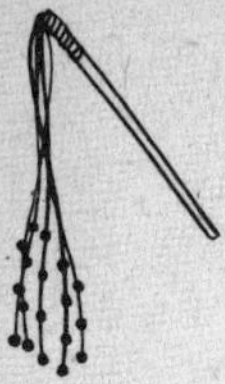

Let us imagine that we are with our Lady as she hears the news of the scourging of her Son. Let us weep with her, and say to her:

HAIL MARY, FULL OF GRACE,
hearing about your Son's sufferings.

THE LORD IS WITH THEE,
united to your soul through love.

BLESSED ART THOU AMONG WOMEN,
because you love us so much as to be willing to suffer for us with Jesus.

BLESSED IS THE FRUIT OF THY WOMB, JESUS.
whose flesh was torn for our sins of the flesh.

HOLY MARY, MOTHER OF GOD, PRAY FOR US SINNERS, NOW, AND AT THE HOUR OF OUR DEATH. AMEN.

THE CROWNING WITH THORNS

Let us imagine that we are present with our Lady as she is told about the soldiers mocking Jesus and crowning him with thorns. Let us try to comfort her and praise her goodness, by saying to her:

HAIL MARY, FULL OF GRACE,
suffering until your heart is breaking.

THE LORD IS WITH THEE,
as you see in your mind every insult and blow.

BLESSED ART THOU AMONG WOMEN,
Because you gave the Son of God his body, through which he suffered to redeem us.

BLESSED IS THE FRUIT OF THY WOMB, JESUS.
suffering the pain of the thorns for our sins of the mind.

HOLY MARY, MOTHER OF GOD, PRAY FOR US SINNERS, NOW, AND AT THE HOUR OF OUR DEATH. AMEN.

THE CARRYING OF THE CROSS

Let us imagine that we are with our Lady as she meets her Son on the road to Calvary and as she sees his sufferings with her own eyes. Let us praise her and say to her:

HAIL MARY, FULL OF GRACE,
scarcely able to look on the bruised wounded body of your Son.

THE LORD IS WITH THEE,
before your eyes as he struggles in pain to the top of Calvary.

BLESSED ART THOU AMONG WOMEN,
because Christ's body, suffering under the cross, came from you.

BLESSED IS THE FRUIT OF THY WOMB, JESUS.
carrying his cross in agony so that we may reach heaven.

HOLY MARY, MOTHER OF GOD, PRAY FOR US SINNERS, NOW, AND AT THE HOUR OF OUR DEATH. AMEN.

THE CRUCIFIXION AND DEATH OF OUR LORD

Let us imagine that we are present with Mary on Calvary as she watches her Son being nailed to the cross, hanging there for three hours, and dying. Let us speak to her in her sorrow and say to her:

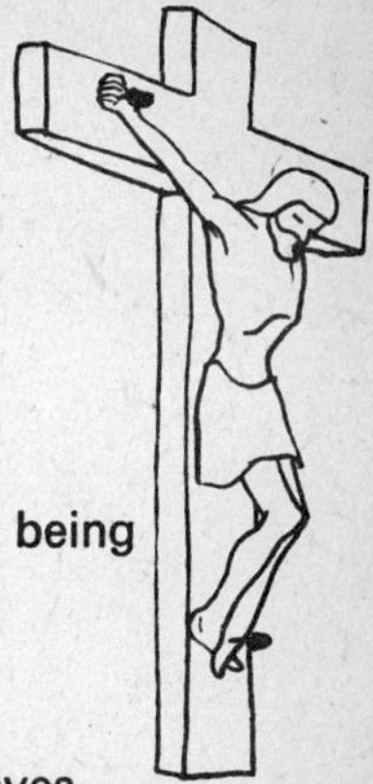

HAIL MARY, FULL OF GRACE,
watching your Son die and not being able to help him.

THE LORD IS WITH THEE,
hanging in agony before your eyes.

BLESSED ART THOU AMONG WOMEN
because you do not ask him to come down.

BLESSED IS THE FRUIT OF THY WOMB, JESUS.
because through this suffering he is opening heaven for us.

HOLY MARY, MOTHER OF GOD, PRAY FOR US SINNERS, NOW, AND AT THE HOUR OF OUR DEATH. AMEN.

THE RESURRECTION

Let us imagine that we are with our Lady when Jesus comes to her after he arose from the dead. Let us share in her happiness and praise her as we say to her:

HAIL MARY, FULL OF GRACE,
full of joy as you meet the risen Christ.

THE LORD IS WITH THEE,
appearing to you and speaking to you again now.

BLESSED ART THOU AMONG WOMEN,
because your Son has risen and turned your sorrow into joy.

BLESSED IS THE FRUIT OF THY WOMB, JESUS.
gloriously arisen, never more to suffer and showing us that he is God.

HOLY MARY, MOTHER OF GOD, PRAY FOR US SINNERS, NOW, AND AT THE HOUR OF OUR DEATH. AMEN.

THE ASCENSION

Let us imagine that we are with Mary, on the first Ascension Thursday, as, with the apostles, she says goodbye to Jesus, and watches him leave this earth and go back to heaven. Let us say these words of praise to her:

HAIL MARY, FULL OF GRACE,
happy as you watch him return to heaven, and a little bit lonely too.

THE LORD IS WITH THEE,
face to face now for the last time in this world.

BLESSED ART THOU AMONG WOMEN,
because you see your Son returning to his glory.

BLESSED IS THE FRUIT OF THY WOMB, JESUS.
returning to heaven after redeeming us and giving his sacraments to the apostles.

HOLY MARY, MOTHER OF GOD, PRAY FOR US SINNERS, NOW, AND AT THE HOUR OF OUR DEATH. AMEN.

THE DESCENT OF THE HOLY GHOST

Let us imagine that we are sitting together with the apostles and our Lady in the room in Jerusalem when the Holy Ghost came to them, giving them the wisdom and courage to start spreading the Church. Let us praise our Lady and say to her:

HAIL MARY, FULL OF GRACE,
helping the Church then as you do now.

THE LORD IS WITH THEE,
in your soul through the grace of the Holy Ghost.

BLESSED ART THOU AMONG WOMEN,
Mother of the Church as well as Mother of Jesus.

BLESSED IS THE FRUIT OF THY WOMB, JESUS.
sending the Holy Ghost to guide and protect the Church.

HOLY MARY, MOTHER OF GOD, PRAY FOR US SINNERS, NOW, AND AT THE HOUR OF OUR DEATH. AMEN.

THE ASSUMPTION

Let us imagine that we are watching, as God takes our Lady, body and soul, up to heaven, there to be happy for ever. Let us praise her and say to her:

HAIL MARY, FULL OF GRACE,
and of glory and happiness for ever united again to your Son.

THE LORD IS WITH THEE,
your Son showing himself to you now as your God.

BLESSED ART THOU AMONG WOMEN,
because your body has already risen, and gone to heaven.

BLESSED IS THE FRUIT OF THY WOMB, JESUS.
glorifying your body from which his body came.

HOLY MARY, MOTHER OF GOD, PRAY FOR US SINNERS, NOW, AND AT THE HOUR OF OUR DEATH. AMEN.

THE CROWNING OF OUR LADY QUEEN OF HEAVEN

Let us imagine that we are watching Jesus raise up his Mother in heaven to the highest place, next to himself, above all the angels and saints. Let us praise her and say to her:

HAIL MARY, FULL OF GRACE,
and of glory and of honour.

THE LORD IS WITH THEE,
crowning you Queen of heaven.

BLESSED ART THOU AMONG WOMEN,
above all the angels and saints,

BLESSED IS THE FRUIT OF THY WOMB, JESUS.
for this honour came to you because he is God.

HOLY MARY, MOTHER OF GOD, PRAY FOR US SINNERS, NOW, AND AT THE HOUR OF OUR DEATH. AMEN.

Another way of praying the Rosary

The previous pages try to show you a way of thinking about the mysteries of the Rosary, while actually using the words of the Hail Mary.

To help you understand better the full meaning of the Rosary, it is a good thing sometimes to break up the Hail Mary into phrases. By repeating each short phrase ten times before going on to the next, you will get to understand the meaning far more easily than when your mind is trying to move from phrase to phrase as you say the Hail Mary in the ordinary way.

In more detail, this is how you can do this:

Open your book at the mystery you are going to say, and hold it in such a way that your eye can glance now and again at the notes that you will find there for each phrase.

Repeat ten times, "Hail Mary, full of grace", imagining yourself present with our Lady in that mystery and calling on her to attract her attention.

Then repeat ten times, "The Lord is with thee", remembering in your mind what these words mean in the particular mystery you are praying about—they will have a different meaning in each mystery.

Then repeat ten times the words, "Blessed art thou amongst women", praising our Lady for the gifts and graces our Lord God gave her in each particular mystery.

Then repeat ten times, "Blessed is the fruit of thy womb, Jesus" (or for a change, "Blessed is your Son, Jesus", or "Blessed is Jesus, the fruit of your womb"), praising our Lord for all he did in the mystery you are thinking about.

And so on with the rest--repeat ten times each of the phrases "Holy Mary, Mother of God, pray for us sinners" and "Now, and at the hour of our death", keeping before your mind the graces you are asking for yourself and others.

PRAYERS OF ST AUGUSTINE

DEVOTION TO GOD

O Lord Jesus, let me know myself, let me know you
and desire nothing else but only you.
Let me hate myself and love you
and do all things for the sake of you.
Let me humble myself and exalt you
and think of nothing but only you.
Let me die to myself and live in you
and take whatever happens as coming from you.
Let me forget myself, and walk after you
and ever desire to follow you.
Let me flee from myself and turn to you
so that I may merit to be defended by you.
Let me fear for myself, let me fear you,
and be amongst those who are chosen by you.
Let me distrust myself and trust in you
and always pray for the love of you.
Let me cling to nothing but only to you.
Look upon me that I may love you.
Call me that I may see you
and forever possess you. Amen.

PRAYER FOR A FRIEND

O sweet Lord Jesus, give him
a heart to love you,
a will to choose you,
a memory to remember you,
a mind to think of you,
a soul which may always be united to you;
And may you, the God of love and mercy,
love him for ever. Amen.

PRAYER FOR HOPE

I beg of you, my God,
let me know you and love you,
so that I may be happy in you.
And though I cannot do this fully in this life,
Yet let me improve from day to day,
till I may do so to the full.
Let me know you more and more in this life,
that I may know you perfectly in heaven.
Let me know you more and more here,
so that I may love you perfectly there,
so that my joy may be great in itself here
and complete in heaven with you.
O truthful God, let me receive
the happiness of heaven which you promise
so that my joy may be full.
In the meantime,
let my mind think of it,
let my tongue talk of it,
let my heart long for it,
let my mouth speak of it,
let my soul hunger after it,
let my flesh thirst after it,
let my whole being desire it,
until such time as I may enter through death
into the joy of my Lord,
there to continue for ever,
world without end. Amen.

PRAYER IN HONOUR OF THE PASSION

O Lord Jesus Christ, who to save all men,
was born, circumcised,
rejected by the Jews,
bound with chains,
led like an innocent lamb to sacrifice,
shamefully brought before Annas and Caiaphas,
before Pilate and Herod,
accused by false witnesses,
beaten with whips,
hit upon the head,
insulted, spat upon,
crowned with thorns,
struck with a reed,
blindfolded and mocked,
stripped of your clothes,
fastened with nails to the cross,
lifted up in the company of thieves,
made to drink gall and vinegar,
and wounded with a spear.

Oh! by all these sacred sufferings,
deliver me, Lord, from the pains of hell,
and lead me to heaven
where you led the good thief who was crucified
by your side. Amen.

PRAYER AFTER TURNING FROM SIN

Too late have I known you,
O everlasting truth.
Too late have I loved you,
O beauty always old and ever new.

Behold you were within,
and I looked for you elsewhere
and in my weakness I ran after the beauty
in the things you have made.

You were with me and I was not with you.
The things you created kept me far from you.
You have called. You have cried out,
and have pierced my deafness.
You have shone forth,
and have lifted my blindness.
You have sent forth your sweetness,
and I have longed after you
and looked for you.
I have tasted you,
and hunger after you.

And now my whole hope is in nothing else
but in your very great mercy,
O Lord, my God.

For he does not really love you,
who loves anything else,
which he does not love for your sake.

O Love, which always burns and never grows less,
true Charity, my God, set me all on fire.
Give me what you command,
and command what you wish.

All-powerful God,
you care for each one of us
as if you loved him alone,
and you care for all,
as if all were but one.

Things of this world pass away
that others may replace them,
But you never pass away,
or never depart.

O God our Father, supremely good,
Beauty of all things beautiful,
to you we entrust
whatsoever we have received from you,
through Jesus Christ our Lord. Amen.

PRAYERS OF CARDINAL NEWMAN

PRAYER FOR PEACE OF HEART

Most sacred, most loving Heart of Jesus,
hidden in the Holy Eucharist,
you beat for us still.
You say, as you said when you lived,
"My delight is to be with the children of men."

When you come to live within me,
make my heart beat with your Heart:
make my soul free from all that is earthly,
all that is hard and cruel,
all that is proud and sensual,
all badness, disorder and death.

Fill my heart with your presence,
so that nothing can disturb me,
but that in your love and your fear,
I may have peace.

PRAYER FOR A HAPPY DEATH

O Lord and Saviour,
help me in my last hour by your sacraments,
and the sweetness of your grace.
Let your words of absolution be said over me;
let the holy oil of extreme unction sign and save me;
and let your holy body and blood be my food.
And let your Mother come to me,
and my guardian angel whisper peace to me,
and your glorious saints and my own dear

patrons smile on me,
that in them,
and through them all,
I may die as I desire to live,
in your Church, in your faith,
and in your holy love. Amen.

PRAYER OF TRUST

My God, you have created me to do you some definite service.
You have given some work to me, which you have not given to any other.
I have my place in your plan.
I may never know what it is in this life,
but I will be told it in the next.

Therefore I will trust you in all things.
If I am sick, my sickness may serve you.
If I am worried, my worry may serve you.
If I am in sorrow, my sorrow may serve you.
You do nothing in vain; you know what you are doing.
You may take away my friends;
you may put me among strangers,
you may make me feel forgotten,
you may make my spirits sink,
you may hide my future from me
—still, you know what you are doing,
and I trust you.

PRAYER FOR GRACE TO HELP OTHERS

Dear Jesus help me to spread your sweet joy everywhere.
Fill my soul with your spirit and life.

Come into me and make my whole being so
completely yours
that all my life may shine like yours.

Shine through me and stay in me
in such a way that every soul I meet may feel
your presence in my soul.
Let them look up and see no longer me,
but only Jesus.

Stay with me and then I will shine as you shine.
I wish to shine so as to be a light to others;
the light, O Jesus, will be all from you,
none of it will be mine;
it will be you shining on others through me.

Thus let me praise you in the way you love best,
by shining on those around me.
Let me preach without preaching,
not by words but by my example,
by the loving influence of what I do,
by the evident love my heart bears to you. Amen.

PRAYERS OF ARCHBISHOP GOODIER

ACT OF OFFERING

Jesus Christ,
My heart is hungry,
Hungry not to have but to give.
I know my emptiness, my uselessness.
I know my failure to do anything well.
I know the waste in every day.
I search around, seeking for I know not what.
But I trust in you in whom I believe.
You have your reasons for everything.
Your measure of work is not ours.
Your judgments are not ours.
Your plans are not ours.
And yours are best, better than ours.
You bring forth fruit as you please,
And when you please,
And in what way you please.
It is enough that I wait, doing what I can.
I desire to belong to you.
Let the rest be as you wish.

PRAYER OF DESIRE FOR UNION WITH GOD

Jesus Christ, I want you—
I want you for my own sake, because
I am so weak,
I am a sinner,
I am nothing.
I want you for your sake

so that I may know you,
so that I may love you,
so that I may become like you.
I want you for the sake of others,
so that I may do them no harm,
so that I may do them only good,
so that I may give you to them.

Jesus Christ, you want me—
you want me for my own sake,
because you made me,
because you died for me,
because you love me.
You want me for your sake,
that I may be your joy,
that I may be your crown,
that I may be one with you.
You want me for the sake of others,
that through me you may heal others,
that through me you may teach others,
that through me you may give yourself to them.

Jesus Christ, you shall have me
all that I have,
all that I am,
all that I possibly can be . . .

SORROW FOR SIN

My God, you know sin, and hate it,
and must condemn it;
In some way I do not understand,
it does hurt you.
Yet you love the sinner and desire to save him.

Here am I, a poor sinner.
I must confess my guilt,
far more offensive than I know.
Let me be true.
Let me not deceive myself or be deceived.
Give me the sense of shame
that should follow my guilt.

Give me the sorrow which will humble me
when I remember
my weakness in yielding,
my giving in to sinful pleasure,
my choosing of evil,
my desire for wrong,
my pride, my temper, my meanness, my shame,
the soul that might have been so beautiful,
spoilt!
The character that might have been so noble,
spoilt!
The powers that might have been so fruitful!
The life that might have been so perfect!
The good that might have been done!
The harm instead that I have done!

Jesus who loves me so,
yet who was so needlessly insulted!
Jesus who bled to death for me,
and I do not care!
Jesus who will yet take me if I come!
I have done nothing for you,
I am doing nothing.
Jesus, Son of David, have mercy on me.

PRAYER IN PRAISE OF CHRIST'S MERCY

You stood to be baptised with sinners at the Jordan,
as one of them you fasted in the desert,
as one of them you were tempted.

You were a friend to the timid Nicodemus.
You were a friend to the Samaritan woman,
telling her of her own sins,
making her confession for her.
You were a friend to her friends.

You let the men of your own town despise you.
You called to yourself the sinful Levi.
You dined with him and his friends,
till self-respecting men were scandalised,
saying,
"Why does he dine with publicans and sinners?"

You were a friend to Mary Magdalen,
saying of her, "Many sins are forgiven her,
because she has loved much."
And saying to her,
"Go in peace. Your faith has made you safe."

You were a friend to the adulteress,
shaming her accusers,
saying, "Neither will I accuse you.
Go now and sin no more."
You were a friend to the rich young man
who refused to follow you.
You looked on him and loved him.
You were a friend to the publican Zacchaeus,
choosing to stay at his house.

You were a friend to Judas who betrayed you,
calling him by his name,
calling him "Friend".
You were a friend to Peter who denied you.
You were a friend to Pilate who condemned you.
You were a friend to the thief who cursed you,
winning him to grace,
saying to him,
"This day you shall be with me in paradise."

You were a friend to all men,
saying to them,
"Come to me all you that labour and are burdened, and I will refresh you."

PRAYER TO OUR LADY

You were conceived without sin,
and no one knew.
The angel saluted you, "Full of grace,"
and not a soul knew.
He said that the Lord was with you,
told you you would be Mother of God
and not even Joseph knew.

Elizabeth saluted you,
"Blessed among women,"
yet you were only a child from Nazareth,
of which place men said,
"Can any good come out of Nazareth?"

Men thought they knew you,
you seemed so easy to know.
They boasted, "His Mother, do we not know her?"
Yet how little did they know!
You called yourself only
"the Handmaid of the Lord,"
content to be no more,
yet how much more you are,
Whom "all generations shall call blessed".

PRAISE OF GOD'S LOVE IN THE BLESSED SACRAMENT

You loved me from all eternity,
therefore you created me.
You loved me after you had made me,
therefore you became man for me.
You loved me after you became man for me,
therefore you lived and died for me.
You loved me after you had died for me,
therefore you rose again for me.
You loved me after you had risen for me,
therefore you went to prepare a place for me.

You loved me
After you had gone to prepare a place for me,
therefore you came back to me.
You loved me after you had come back to me,
therefore you desire to enter into me
and be united to me.
This is the meaning of the Blessed Sacrament.
the mystery of love.

AN ACT OF DESIRE

My God, I desire you and your love.
My poor heart longs for peace of mind.
It longs to be at peace with you.
It longs to be at peace with all men.
It longs to be at perfect peace within itself.
And this you alone can give me,
the peace of sinlessness,
the peace of selflessness,
of doing my whole duty,
with no giving in to self-love,
in whatever form it may hide itself;
The peace of knowing, loving and serving you,
of knowing that I belong to you,
and that I shall belong to you for ever.

PRAYER OF LOVE FOR JESUS CHRIST

Jesus Christ, close beside me,
here and now,
the same now as in Jerusalem and Galilee,
looking at me with your loving eyes,
longing to have me for your very own.
Feeling for me with your tender heart,
desiring to give me what is best for me,
yet meek and humble,
waiting for me,
for you will not force yourself upon me,
waiting for me to make the first step,
waiting till I ask you to come to me,
Jesus Christ,
I believe in you, I love you,

I trust in you, I want you,
I give myself to you.
Give yourself to me,
Come, Lord Jesus! Come quickly!

PRAYERS OF ADORATION, CONFIDENCE AND OFFERING

RESIGNATION TO GOD'S WILL

What is to happen to me today, O my God?
I do not know.
I only know that nothing will happen to me
which you have not foreseen, permitted or
arranged from all eternity.
That is enough for me to know, O my God.

I adore your eternal plan.
I submit to it with all my heart for love of you.
I wish for all,
I accept all,
I offer to you the sacrifice of all,
and I unite this sacrifice to that of Jesus Christ,
my divine Saviour.
I ask you,
in his name and through his merits,
for patience in my sufferings;
I ask you for that perfect obedience
which we owe you in everything which you will
or permit to happen. Amen.
(Père Surin, S.J.)

GOD'S WILL BE DONE

Rule all by your wisdom, O Lord,
so that my soul may always serve you according
to your will,
and not as I may choose.
Do not punish me, I beg of you,

by granting that which I wish or ask
if it offends your love,
because I desire your love to live always in my soul.
Let me deny myself, so that I may serve you.
Let me live for you, who in yourself are the true life. Amen.
(St Teresa.)

THANKS BE TO GOD

Thanks be to God for the light and the darkness,
Thanks be to God for the winds that blow
Thanks be to God for the shower and the sunshine
Thanks be to God for all things that grow.

Thanks be to God for the lightning and storm
Thanks be to God for joy and for sorrow,
Thanks be to God for his own great goodness,
Thanks be to God that what is, is so.

Thanks be to God when the harvest is plenty
Thanks be to God when the gardens are low
Thanks be to God when our pockets are empty,
Thanks be to God when again they o'erflow.

TRUST HIM

Trust him when dark doubts attack you,
Trust him when your strength is small,
Trust him when to simply trust him
Is the hardest thing of all.

Trust him, he is ever faithful,
Trust him for his will is best.
Trust him for the Heart of Jesus,
Is the only place of rest.

Trust him then, through doubts and sunshine,
All your cares upon him cast,
Till the storm of life is over,
And your trusting days are past.

ACT OF CONFIDENCE

O sweet and tender God,
I leave in your hands my hopes and my fears,
my likes and my dislikes,
my happiness and my unhappiness,
my sorrows and my joys.
To you I offer the needs of my mortal body
and the more important needs of my immortal soul.
I need have no fear for my soul
while I do not take it away from your loving care.

Though my faults and my misery are great,
my hope in you is greater still.
It is greater than my weakness,
greater than my difficulties,
stronger than death.

Though temptation should attack me,
I will hope in you.
Though I may fall under my weakness,
I will still hope in you.
Even though I may break my promises,
I will look to you confidently
for grace to make and keep them again.
Though you may take away my life,
even then will I trust in you,
for you are my Father, my God,
the support of my salvation.
You are my kind, my tender and loving Father;

I am your loving child,
and I throw myself into your arms and beg your blessing.
I put my trust in you,
and so trusting, I will not be confounded. Amen.
(Blessed Claude de la Colombiere.)

OBEDIENCE TO GOD'S WILL

Give me, Lord,
knowledge of your will in all things,
both small and great;
give me grace to choose it, to follow it,
and to love it at all costs,
simply because it is yours,
that so I may please you. Amen.

PRAYER OF TRUST

If you wish me to be in darkness,
may you be blessed.
If you wish me to be in light,
may you be blessed again.
If you are pleased to comfort me,
may you be blessed.
And if it is your will to punish me,
may you also be equally blessed.
Keep me from all sin,
and I will fear neither death nor hell.
So long as you do not throw me aside,
or shut me out from heaven,
no suffering that comes to me will hurt;
because in all things I place my trust in you,
O Sacred Heart of Jesus.

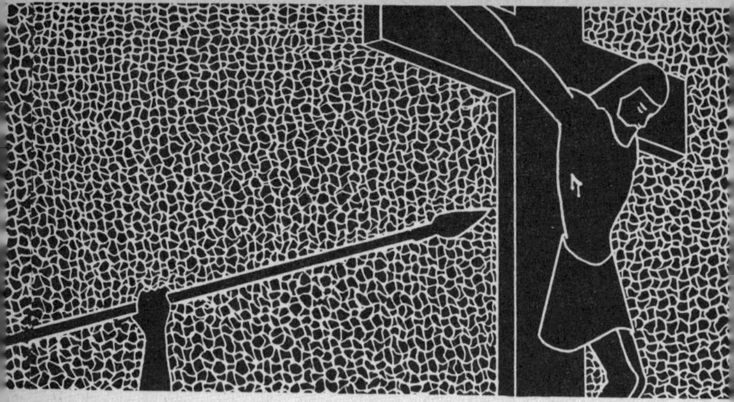

PRAYERS TO OUR LORD AND HIS SACRED HEART

PRAYER FOR HELP

(Based on our Lord's words on the cross.)

Divine Jesus, Son of God made man,
who for our salvation was pleased to be born in a stable,
to pass your life in poverty, trials and misery,
and to die in the sufferings of the cross,
I beg of you to help me.

Dear Lord,
say to your divine Father at the hour of my death,
"Father forgive him";
say to your beloved Mother, "Behold your son";

say to my soul, "This day you will be with me in paradise." My God, my God, do not forsake me in that hour.

I thirst, yes, my God, my soul thirsts after you,
who are the fountain of living waters.
My life passes like a shadow;
in a little while all will be ended.
Therefore, O my adorable Saviour,
from this moment, and for all eternity,
into your hands I commend my spirit;
Lord Jesus receive my soul.

O JESUS, LIVING IN MARY

O Jesus, living in Mary,
come and live in your servants,
in the spirit of your holiness,
in the fulness of your power,
in the truth of your virtues,
in the perfection of your ways,
in the sharing of your mysteries,
overcome every power of the enemy,
in your Spirit, for the glory of the Father. Amen.
(Fr Olier.)

PETITIONS TO JESUS

Jesus, Son of the Eternal Father, convert me.
Jesus, Son of Mary, take me as her child.
Jesus, my master, teach me.
Jesus, prince of peace, give me peace.
Jesus, my refuge, receive me.
Jesus, my shepherd, feed my soul.

Jesus, model of patience, comfort me.
Jesus, meek and humble of heart, make me like you.
Jesus, my redeemer, save me.
Jesus, my God and my all, possess me.
Jesus, the true way, guide me.
Jesus, eternal truth, teach me.
Jesus, life of the saints, make me live in you.
Jesus, my support, give me strength.
Jesus, my justice, make me good.
Jesus, healer of my soul, heal me.
Jesus, my judge, pardon me.
Jesus, my king, rule me.
Jesus, my holiness, make me holy.
Jesus, infinite goodness, pardon me.
Jesus, living bread from heaven, be the food of my soul.
Jesus, my helper, help me.
Jesus, magnet of love, draw me.
Jesus, my protector, defend me.
Jesus, my hope, support me.
Jesus, object of my love, unite me to yourself.
Jesus, fountain of life, refresh me.
Jesus, my divine victim, atone for me.
Jesus, my last end, let me possess you.
Jesus, my glory, glorify me.
Amen.

JESUS HELP ME

In every need let me come to you with humble trust, saying, Jesus, help me.

In all my doubts, temptations and troubles of mind, Jesus, help me.

When I am lonely or tired, Jesus, help me.

When my plans and hopes have failed, in all my disappointments and sorrows, Jesus, help me.

When others let me down, and your grace alone can assist me, Jesus, help me.

When my heart is heavy with failure and when I see no good come from my efforts, Jesus, help me.

When I feel impatient, and when my cross is hard to carry, Jesus, help me.

When I am ill, and my head and hands cannot work, Jesus, help me.

Always, always, in spite of weakness and falls of every kind, Jesus, help me and never leave me. Amen.

PRAYERS FROM THE GOSPELS

I am a sinful man, O Lord, I have sinned before heaven and against you. I am not worthy to be called your son.

O God, be merciful to me a sinner. If you will, you can make me clean. You who take away the sins of the world, have mercy on me.

Lord, I have sought you sorrowing. To whom shall I go? You have the words of eternal life, and I have believed and have known that you are the Christ, the Son of God, who are come into this world.

Master, I will follow you wherever you go, I will lay down my life for you. Lord, you know all things, you know that I love you. Amen.

BEADS OF THE SACRED HEART
(To be said on ordinary rosary beads.)

On the large beads say—

"Sacred Heart of Jesus,
make my heart like yours."

On the small beads say—

"Sweet Heart of Jesus, be my love."

RABBONI (MASTER)

When I am dying, how glad I shall be
That the lamp of my life has been burned out for thee;
That sorrow has darkened my path every day;
That thorns and not roses were spread on the way.
That sorrow of spirit so often was mine,
Since sorrow of spirit so often was thine.
My beloved Rabboni, how glad I shall be,
To die with the hope of a welcome from thee.

ST PATRICK'S BREASTPLATE

I rise up today,
The power of God directing me,
The strength of God supporting me,
The wisdom of God guiding me,
The eye of God looking before me,
The ear of God listening to me,
The hand of God protecting me,

The way of God stretching out before me,
The shield of God defending me,
The angels of God guarding me,
against snares of devils,
against temptations of vices,
against inclinations of nature,
against everyone who will wish evil to me.

Christ with me, Christ before me, Christ behind me,
Christ in me, Christ beneath me, Christ above me,
Christ on my right hand, Christ on my left hand,
Christ where I sit, Christ where I arise,
Christ in the heart of everyone who thinks of me,
Christ in the mouth of everyone who speaks of me,
Christ in every eye that sees me,
Christ in every ear that hears me.

AN ACT OF PERFECT LOVE

O God, I love you for yourself
And not that I may heaven gain,
Nor yet that they who love you not
Must suffer hell's eternal pain.

O Jesus, suffering on the cross,
Your love had me in mind;
For me you bore the nails and spear
And shame of every kind.

And griefs and torments numberless,
And sweat of agony;
Even death itself, and all for one
Who was your enemy.

Then why, O dearest Jesus Christ,
Should I not love you well;
Not for the sake of winning heaven
Nor of escaping hell.

Not with any hope of gain,
Not seeking a reward;
But just as you have loved me,
O ever-loving Lord.

Even so I love you, and will love,
And in your praise will sing;
Solely because you are my God
And my eternal King.
(St Francis Xavier.)

O JESUS, HIDDEN GOD

O Jesus, hidden God, I cry to you;
O Jesus, hidden love, I run to you;
With all the strength I have I worship you;
With all the love I have I cling to you;
With all my soul I long to be with you.

O Jesus, never ending love, who seeks me,
You who died for longing love of me,
King, in all your beauty, come to me,
White-robed, blood-sprinkled Jesus, come to me,
And go no more, dear Lord, away from me.

O sweetest Jesus, bring me home to you,
Free me, dearest Lord, from all but you.
From all the chains that keep me back from you;
Call me, most powerful love, I'll follow you;
You are my all, and I love only you.

O hidden love, who now is loving me,
O wounded love, who once was dead to me;
O patient love, who wearies not of me—
O bear with me, till I am lost in you;
O bear with me, till I am found in you. Amen.

PRAYER TO THE SACRED HEART FOR LOVE

O Heart of God, which reaches out so tenderly to the hearts of men; O Heart, that watches over us and loves us as a mother loves her earliest born, give us hearts such as you long for us to have, hearts that are strong to dare, that are brave to bear, and willing to forgive. Take these little hearts of ours and throw them into the burning flames of your own infinite love.

There, in those healing fires, they will learn life's best, because truest lesson. Although the cure be a hard one, yet in the end, when the strength of temptation has been weakened by the cleansing fires of your heart's great love, we shall have received a peace that nothing can take away. Heart all patient, all good, all full of pity for our human weakness, have mercy on us.

ACT OF TRUST IN THE SACRED HEART

My Lord and my God, I believe all you have ever taught.

There is nothing harder for me to believe than that you love someone as sinful and worthless as I am; but I do believe it, Lord,

and therefore, O Sacred Heart of Jesus, I place all my trust in you.

I believe that you have loved me with an everlasting love,
and therefore, O Sacred Heart of Jesus, I place all my trust in you.

I believe that your love for me is as tender as a mother's love,
and therefore, O Sacred Heart of Jesus, I place all my trust in you.

I believe that you have planned, lovingly and wisely, everything which will ever happen to me,
and therefore, O Sacred Heart of Jesus, I place all my trust in you.

I will never seek pleasure forbidden by you because you know what is bad for me and what is good,
and I trust in you, O Sacred Heart of Jesus.

I will always pray, "May your holy will be done in all things,"
because I trust in you, O Sacred Heart of Jesus.

I will accept the sorrows of life as I accept the joys, with a thankful heart,
because I trust in you, O Sacred Heart of Jesus.

I will not be worried or anxious about anything,
because I trust in you, O Sacred Heart of Jesus.

I will never lose heart in my efforts to be good,
because I trust in you, O Sacred Heart of Jesus.

However weak or sinful I may be, I will never doubt your mercy,
because I trust in you, O Sacred Heart of Jesus.

In all my temptations, I place my trust in you,
O Sacred Heart of Jesus.
In all my weakness, I place my trust in you,
O Sacred Heart of Jesus.
In all my difficulties, I place my trust in you,
O Sacred Heart of Jesus.
In all my trials, I place my trust in you,
O Sacred Heart of Jesus.
In all my sorrows, I place my trust in you,
O Sacred Heart of Jesus.
In all my work, I place my trust in you,
O Sacred Heart of Jesus.
In every failure, I place my trust in you,
O Sacred Heart of Jesus.
In every discouragement, I place my trust in you,
O Sacred Heart of Jesus.
In life and in death, I place my trust in you,
O Sacred Heart of Jesus.
In time and eternity, I place my trust in you,
O Sacred Heart of Jesus.

PRAYER OF LOVE

O Heart of Jesus, I desire to unite myself to you and to possess you so that I no longer live except in you who will be my dwelling place for all eternity.
In you, O most lovable Heart, I desire to love and work and suffer. Take away from me, therefore, all that is of self. In its place put yourself, and change me so as to be like you. May I no longer live except by you and for you.
Be therefore my life, my love and my all.
(St Margaret Mary.)

PRAYER BASED ON THE TWELVE PROMISES

Heart of Jesus, give us all the graces necessary for our state in life ; you have promised it, O Jesus.

Heart of Jesus, give peace to our families ;
you have promised it, O Jesus.

Heart of Jesus, comfort us in all our sorrows ;
you have promised it, O Jesus.

Heart of Jesus, be our protection during life,
and above all at the hour of our death ;
you have promised it, O Jesus.

Heart of Jesus, give your blessing to all our works ;
you have promised it, O Jesus.

Heart of Jesus, be merciful to sinners ;
you have promised it, O Jesus.

Heart of Jesus, make sinful souls holy ;
you have promised it, O Jesus.

Heart of Jesus, make holy souls more holy ;
you have promised it, O Jesus.

Heart of Jesus, bless the house where your
picture is exposed and honoured ;
you have promised it, O Jesus.

Heart of Jesus, give to priests the power of
changing the most sinful hearts ;
you have promised it, O Jesus.

Heart of Jesus, remember for ever the names of
those who make others love you ;
you have promised it, O Jesus.

Heart of Jesus, give those who receive Holy Communion on nine consecutive First Fridays the grace of final perseverance, so that they may not die as your enemies but strengthened by your sacraments; may you be their sure protection at their last hour; you have promised it, O Jesus.

ACT OF CONSECRATION TO THE SACRED HEART

Most sweet Jesus, redeemer of the human race, look down upon us humbly kneeling before your altar.

We belong to you, and we desire to remain yours for ever.

In order that we may be more strongly united to you,
each one of us here today freely offers himself to your most Sacred Heart.

Many indeed have never known you;
many have disobeyed your commandments and rejected you.
Have mercy on them all, most merciful Jesus, and draw them all to your most Sacred Heart.

O Lord, be the king of those who have turned their backs on you, as well as of those who have never left you.
Grant that they may return to their Father's house, so that they will not lose their souls by sin.

O Lord, be the king of those who have been led astray by error, and who are separated from you. Bring them back to the one true Church, so that soon there may be one fold and one shepherd.

O Lord, be the king also of all those who have no religion. Deliver them out of the darkness into the light and kingdom of God.

Grant to your Church, O Lord, freedom and security;
give peace and good government to all nations;
make the earth ring out from end to end with one voice, saying,
"Praise to the divine Heart, which has brought about our salvation. To him be glory and honour for ever."

THE LOVING THOUGHT OF JESUS

JESU DULCIS MEMORIA

The loving thought of Jesus brings
True joy to every human heart,
But greater joy than even this,
His gracious presence brings to us.

No clearer tune is ever sung,
No gentler word is ever heard,
No sweeter thought can fill our mind,
Than, "Jesus Christ, the Son of God."

O Jesus, hope of penitents,
How kind you are when asked for help,
How good to those who seek yourself,
But more to those who find you.

Our human words can never tell,
Nor can our language ever state,
What loving Jesus really means,
He only knows who truly loves.

They who taste, desire him more,
And they who drink thirst more for him,
Naught else will satisfy their souls,
Save Jesus, whom they know and love.

O Jesus, Lord, my sweetest king,
My living soul's most precious hope,
With tears of love and prayers of soul,
I long to make you ever mine.

O, always stay with us, dear Lord,
And give us light to guide our way,
Drive out the darkness from our souls,
And fill the world with peace and joy.

O Jesus, Virgin-Mother's child,
O love, you give your sweetness here,
To you be honour and all praise,
On earth and in our heavenly home.

O Jesus, then, be thou our joy,
Who are our future sweet reward,
May all give glory at all times,
While never-ending ages pass.

LITANY TO JESUS CHRIST

Lord, have mercy.
Christ, have mercy.
Lord, have mercy.
Jesus, hear us.
Jesus, graciously hear us.

God the Father of heaven	Have mercy on us.
God the Son, redeemer of the world	"
God the Holy Ghost	"
Holy Trinity, one God	"
Jesus, Son of the living God	"
Jesus, glory of the Father	"
Jesus, brightness of eternal light	"
Jesus, king of heaven	"
Jesus, shining with holiness	"
Jesus, Son of the Virgin Mary	"
Jesus, most lovable	"
Jesus, most admirable	"
Jesus, all-powerful God	"
Jesus, having loving care for our future	"
Jesus, bringing great news	"
Jesus, most powerful	"
Jesus, most patient	"
Jesus, most obedient	"
Jesus, meek and humble of heart	"
Jesus, lover of chastity	"
Jesus, lover of us	"
Jesus, God of peace	"
Jesus, author of life	"
Jesus, model of all virtues	"
Jesus, zealous for souls	"

Jesus, our God	Have mercy on us.
Jesus, our protector	"
Jesus, lover of the poor	"
Jesus, treasure of the faithful	"
Jesus, good shepherd	"
Jesus, true light of our souls	"
Jesus, eternal wisdom	"
Jesus, infinite goodness	"
Jesus, our way and our life	"
Jesus, joy of angels	"
Jesus, king of patriarchs	"
Jesus, master of apostles	"
Jesus, teacher of evangelists	"
Jesus, light of confessors	"
Jesus, purity of virgins	"
Jesus, reward of all the saints	"
Be merciful	Spare us, O Jesus.
Be merciful	Graciously hear us, O Jesus.
From all evil	O Jesus, deliver us.
From all sin	"
From your anger	"
From the snares of the devil	"
From the spirit of impurity	"
From everlasting death	"
From the neglect of your grace	"
Through your holy incarnation	"
Through your nativity	"
Through your infancy	"
Through your most divine life	"
Through your labours	"
Through your agony and passion	"
Through your cross and loneliness	"
Through your weakness	"

Through your death and burial O Jesus, deliver us.
Through your resurrection "
Through your ascension "
Through your joys "
Through your glory "
Lamb of God, you take away the sins of the world Spare us, O Jesus.
Lamb of God, you take away the sins of the world Graciously hear us, O Jesus.
Lamb of God, you take away the sins of the world Have mercy on us, O Jesus.
Jesus hear us
Jesus graciously hear us.

LET US PRAY

O Lord Jesus Christ, who said: Ask and you shall receive; seek, and you shall find; knock, and it shall be opened unto you; grant we beseech you, to us who ask, the gift of your most divine love, that with all our heart, words and works, we may love you, and never cease to praise you.

Give us, O Lord, a perpetual fear and love of your holy name; for you never cease to guide those whom you firmly establish in your love. Amen.

PRAYING TO JESUS CHRIST IN THE GOSPELS

Read a little of the life of our Lord from the Gospels or some other book. Stop after every sentence or two, and address to Jesus the words of any prayer like the following prayer, saying the words slowly and carefully each time and remembering their meaning:

LORD, I BELIEVE IN YOU, HOPE IN YOU, LOVE YOU.
HELP ME TO PLEASE YOU IN ALL THAT I DO.

It is also a very valuable exercise of prayer to say this same prayer in the "Litany of the Holy Name", instead of each "Have mercy on us", or after each thought of the "Rosary Thoughts" on p. 73 ff. In doing this, we first call on Jesus, address some words of praise to him and then express our faith, hope and love and our desire to serve him, in the words of this little prayer.

PRAYERS IN HONOUR OF THE BLESSED SACRAMENT

PRAISE OF COMMUNION
(*SACRUM CONVIVIUM*)

O sacred banquet, in which Christ is received,
the offering of his passion is renewed,
the mind is filled with grace,
and a promise of future glory is given to us!

PRAISE OF BLESSED EUCHARIST
(*LAUDA SION*)

Holy Church now praise your Saviour,
He is your King and Shepherd too,
So praise in songs and hymns.

O praise with all your strength and power,
For he is greater than all praise
Nor can you praise enough.

Remember now his special gift;
The living bread which gives us life
Today is set before us.

No doubt at all remains with us,
At table seated with the twelve,
He gave his loving gift.

Let praise be all complete and loud,
Let hearts be full of joyful praise,
In gladness and respect.

We honour now this glorious day,
And always will recall with love,
The gift he gave us then.

At table of our new-found king,
New paschal meal of new-given law
Put end to all before.

The new law now put old to flight,
The truth now chased the darkness cold,
The light brought end to night.

What Christ then did at this great meal,
He ordered us to do today,
That we remember him.

Obedient to his loving words,
We consecrate the bread and wine,
In sacrifice for sin.

The teaching given Christians is,
The bread into his body is changed,
The wine into his blood.

We cannot understand or see,
But living faith now makes us firm,
Beyond all nature's laws.

Appearances not real, but signs
Of what lies hidden underneath,
Where priceless gift we find.

For food to flesh and drink to blood
Is changed; yet Christ complete remains,
'Neath each appearance true.

He's never broken when received,
He's not divided, torn apart,
    But comes to us entire.

Received by thousands or by one,
By being received he's not destroyed,
    And each receives the same.

Both just and sinners can receive,
But fruits are not the same in each,
    It brings both life and death.

The just get life, the sinners death,
A very different effect,
    Though both received alike.

And when we break the sign of bread,
Remember then and do not doubt,
The same is now in each small part,
    As first the whole contained.

We don't divide our Saviour Christ,
We break the covering sign alone,
The glory or the state of Christ,
    Is not made less at all.

Behold the Bread for angels fit,
Is made the food of mortal men,
It's God's true bread to feed his sons,
    No good for those in sin.

In figures long ago foretold,
When Paschal Lamb the chosen saved,
When Isaac once was sacrificed,
    And manna fed the Jews.

Jesus, Shepherd, Bread most true,
Have mercy now on us your own,
Defend us all and care for us,
And grant that we'll your goodness see
    In everlasting life.

God, you know and rule all things;
You feed us men while here on earth;
In heaven let us share your feast,
Let's be your friends and heirs with you
    In homeland of the saints.

HAIL TO THEE TRUE BODY
(*AVE VERUM CORPUS*)

Hail to thee, true body born
    From the Virgin Mary's womb!
The same that on the cross was nailed
    And bore for man the bitter doom.

Thou, whose side was pierced and flowed
    Both with water and with blood;
Suffer us to taste of thee,
    In our life's last agony.

        O kind, O loving one!
        A sweet Jesus, Mary's Son!

VICTIM SAVING US FROM SIN
(*O SALUTARIS*)

O Victim, saving us from sin,
Who opens heaven's gates to us,
From Satan now temptations come,
    Give strength and bring us health.

To you, one God in persons three,
We offer everlasting praise,
Who'll give us life that never ends,
In heaven our homeland true.

PRAYERS IN HONOUR OF OUR LADY

MOTHER FULL OF SORROW

(*STABAT MATER*)

Mary, full of sorrow, stood
Tearfully beside the cross,
On which hung her only Son.

Full of grief, with him she suffered,
As the sword of bitter sorrow
Pierced her mourning soul with pain.

Oh, how sad and deeply pained
Was the blessed Virgin, Mother
Of the only Son of God.

His dear loving Mother wept
In her sorrow, as she watched
All the pains of Christ her son.

Is there one who would not weep,
Christ's own mother could he see
Bearing such great agony?

Who while watching Christ's dear Mother,
Suffering with her only Son,
Could refuse to mourn with her?

She saw Jesus in his torments,
And his body torn with scourges
For the sins that we commit.

Still, she watched her loving Son,
Torn with pain in soul and body,
Till the moment of his death.

Oh, my Mother, full of love,
Let me share your weight of pain,
So that I may weep with you.

So that I may always please him,
Grant that my poor heart may burn
With the love of Christ my God.

Holy Mother, grant this prayer;
Let the wounds of Jesus Christ,
Firmly in my heart be fixed.

Let me share with you the pain
Of your loving wounded Son,
Freely suffering for me.

Let me weep with you through love
Mourning for the Crucified,
Every day that I will live.

I desire to stand beside you
Near the cross, and take a share
In your weeping and lament.

Virgin of all virgins best,
Show your tenderhearted love;
Let me weep and mourn with you.

Let me bear the cross of Christ.
Let me share with him his passion,
And remember all his wounds.

May his wounds now wound my heart!
May his cross and precious blood,
Take away all selfishness.

Virgin, my poor soul defend
On the judgment day of God,
Lest in fire of hell I burn.

Christ, when I am called to you
Let me, by your Mother's prayers,
Gain the crown of victory.

When my body comes to die,
Grant my soul may reach its home,
In the joys of paradise.

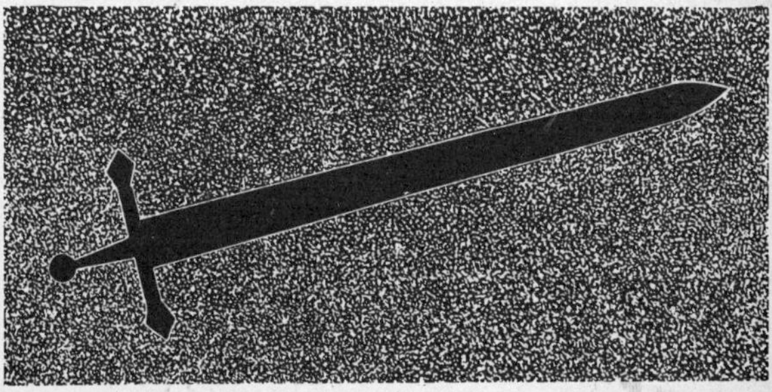

PRAISE OF OUR LADY

You are all beautiful, O Mary,
You were always free from original sin.
You are the glory of Jerusalem.
You are the joy of the people of God.
You are the great honour of our human race.
You are the helper of sinners.
O Mary, O Mary,
Virgin most prudent, Mother most merciful,
Pray to the Lord Jesus Christ for us.

OFFERING TO OUR LADY

Most holy Mary, Virgin Mother of God,
unworthy though I am to be your servant,
yet moved by your motherly care for me
and longing to serve you,
I choose you this day,
in the presence of my guardian angel and all the saints of heaven,
to be my queen, my helper and my mother,
and I firmly resolve to serve you always,
and to do what I can that all may give
faithful service to you.

Therefore, most loving Mother,
through the Precious Blood your Son poured out for me,
I beg you to receive me as your servant forever.
Help me in all my actions,
and beg for me the grace
never, by word or action or thought,
to be displeasing to you or to your most holy Son.

Remember me, dearest Mother,
and do not leave me at the hour of death. Amen.
(St Francis de Sales.)

MEMORARE

Remember, O most loving Virgin Mary,
that never was it known
that anyone who fled to your protection,
begged your help, or looked for your prayers,
was left unaided.
Therefore, full of confidence, I fly to you,

O Virgin of virgins, my Mother;
to you I come,
before you I stand,
sinful and sorrowful;
O Mother of the Word made Flesh,
refuse not my prayers, but in your loving mercy
hear and answer me. Amen.
(St Bernard.)

PRAYER TO OUR LADY FOR A HAPPY DEATH

O most holy Virgin Mary, who stands for ever
before the most holy Trinity;
and to whom it is granted at all times to pray for
us to your most beloved Son;
pray for me in all my needs;
help me, beg and obtain for me the pardon of all my
sins.

Help me especially at my last hour;
and when I can no longer give any sign of the use
of reason,
then let you encourage me,
make the sign of the cross for me,
and fight for me against the enemy.
Make in my name an act of faith;
favour me with a sign of my salvation,
and never let me despair of the mercy of God.

Help me to defeat the wicked enemy.
When I can no longer say, "Jesus, Mary and Joseph,
I place my soul in your hands",
let you say it for me.
When I can no longer hear human words of
consolation, let you comfort me.

Do not leave me before I have been judged,
and if I have to free my soul from sin in purgatory,
O pray for me immediately and without ceasing,
and inspire my friends to pray for me,
so that I may soon enjoy the blessed sight of God.
Lighten my sufferings,
deliver me quickly,
and lead my soul into heaven with you,
so that united with you and all the saints,
I may bless and praise my God for all eternity.
Amen.
(St John Vianney, Curé d'Ars.)

PRAYER IN A PARTICULAR NEED

Say not, merciful Virgin, that you cannot help me; for your beloved Son has given you all power in heaven and on earth.

Say not that you ought not to help me; for you are the mother of all the poor children of Adam, and my mother in particular.

Since then, merciful Virgin, you are my Mother and you are all-powerful, what excuse can you offer if you do not help me?

See, my Mother, see, you are obliged to hear my prayers and to grant me what I ask.
(St Francis de Sales.)

PRAYER FOR SUCCESS IN STUDY

O Mary, Mother of love, of knowledge and of holy hope,

by whose prayers many have grown wise and become holy,
I choose you as the guide and patroness of my studies.

Because of the deep tenderness of your motherly love for me,
and because Jesus, the eternal Wisdom, was pleased to take from you our flesh
and to give you more heavenly light than all the saints,
I humbly ask that you would obtain for me by your prayers the grace of the Holy Ghost.
With this grace may I be able to understand and remember,
and show forth to others by word and action,
all things which bring honour to you and to your Son,
and which will lead me and others to everlasting life. Amen.

PRAYERS IN HONOUR OF THE SEVEN SORROWS OF OUR LADY

Most sorrowful Virgin,
sorrow filled your heart when,
on offering your divine Son in the temple,
holy Simeon told you that a sword would pierce your soul,
and you knew then that you would be asked to suffer with Jesus.
I wish to join with you in this sorrow,
and I ask you, O Queen of Martyrs,
to obtain for me the grace

that I may always remember my death,
which will help to keep me from all sin.

Hail Mary . . .

Most holy and sorrowful Virgin,
sorrow filled your motherly heart when you saw your divine Infant hated by Herod
and you had to flee with him to Egypt to save him.
I wish to join with you in this sorrow,
and ask you, O Queen of Martyrs,
to obtain for me the grace
to avoid all the temptations of my enemies on the difficult road to heaven.

Hail Mary . . .

Most sorrowful Virgin,
sorrow filled your heart when you were separated from your divine Son,
who remained lost for three days in Jerusalem
while you looked everywhere for him.
I wish to join with you in the sorrow you felt then,
and I ask you, O Queen of Martyrs,
to obtain for me the grace never to lose Jesus your Son,
but always to remain united to him by the help of his grace.

Hail Mary . . .

Most sorrowful Mother,
sorrow filled your motherly heart when you followed your dear Son to Calvary,
and saw him falling under the weight of the cross.
I wish to join with you in this sorrow,

and ask you, O Queen of Martyrs,
to obtain for me the grace to bear with patience
whatever cross it will please God to send me.

Hail Mary . . .

Most sorrowful Mother,
the greatest sorrow filled your heart when you stood near the cross of Jesus,
and watched him die in suffering for the sins of the world
without being able to do anything to help him.
I wish to join with you in this sorrow,
and ask you, O Queen of Martyrs,
to obtain for me the grace to fight against all my temptations
even though it costs me effort and suffering and death,
so that strengthened by his love when I am dying,
I may obtain the grace of a happy death.

Hail Mary . . .

Most sorrowful Mother,
sorrow filled your heart when the adorable body of your divine Son
was taken down from the cross and laid in your arms.
I wish to join with you in this sorrow,
and ask you to obtain for me the grace to receive Jesus into my soul before I die,
so that I may be perfectly united to him for ever in heaven.

Hail Mary . . .

Most sorrowful Virgin,
sorrow again filled your heart when the sacred

body of Jesus was taken from your arms and
placed in the grave.
I wish to join with you in this last sorrow of yours,
and ask you to obtain for me,
through the sufferings of Jesus,
which were the cause of all your sorrows,
a sincere sorrow for my sins, a burning love of God,
and a tender and practical devotion towards you.

Hail Mary . . .

PROMISE OF DEVOTION TO OUR LADY

Holy Mary, Mother of God, and Virgin,
I choose you this day as my mother, queen,
patroness and helper.
I firmly resolve and intend never to leave you,
and never to say or do anything against you,
and never to allow anything to be done by others
against your honour.

Receive me therefore, I beg of you,
as your servant for ever;
help me in all my actions,
and do not leave me at the hour of my death.
Amen.
(St John Berchman).

PRAYER FOR MARY'S PROTECTION

We fly to your protection, O holy Mother of God;
do not refuse to hear our prayers in our needs,
but save us from all dangers,
O ever glorious and blessed Virgin.

PRAYERS FOR OTHERS

FOR ONE'S CHILDREN

O heavenly Father, I offer my children to you.
Be their God and Father.
Mercifully make up for whatever, through weakness or neglect, is missing in me.

Strengthen them to overcome the evil of the world, to resist all temptations to sin, and deliver them from the secret traps of the enemy.

Pour your grace into their hearts.
Strengthen and increase in them the gifts of your Holy Spirit.
May they grow daily in grace and in the knowledge of our Lord Jesus Christ.

May they faithfully serve you here on earth,
and may they come to rejoice
in your presence for ever in heaven. Amen.

FOR OUR SPECIAL FRIENDS

O blessed Lord, you have commanded us to love one another.
You have freely given us many gifts of body and soul.
Give us the grace that in loving you and for your sake
we may love everyone else in the world.
We ask your mercy for all,
but especially for the friends whom your love has given us.

Love them, O Fountain of Love,
and make them love you with all their hearts,
so that they may will, and speak, and do
those things only which are pleasing to you. Amen.
(St Anselm.)

FOR A FRIEND

May the grace and blessing of the Sacred Heart be with him.

May the peace of the Sacred Heart surround him.

May the merits of the Sacred Heart plead for him.

May the love of the Sacred Heart set his soul on fire.

May the sorrows of the Sacred Heart comfort him in his troubles.

May the zeal of the Sacred Heart give life to his soul.

May the virtues of the Sacred Heart shine in every word and work of his, and may the joys of heaven be his eternal reward. Amen.

FOR PRIESTS

O Jesus, Priest for ever, keep your priests safe in the shelter of your Sacred Heart, where none may harm them.

Keep clean from sin their anointed hands which touch your sacred body each day, and their lips which drink your precious blood.

Keep pure their hearts, marked with the wonderful marks of the priesthood.

Let your holy love protect them from the sinfulness of the world they work in.

Bless their work with success, and may the souls they work for be a joy to them here in this life, and help them to the reward of everlasting glory in the next life.

Mary, Queen of priests, pray for them, and obtain for us many and holy priests. Amen.

FOR THE MISSIONS

Dear Jesus, you came on earth to save the souls of all mankind.
Yet many have never heard of your holy name.
Have pity on all who do not know that you died for them on the cross.

Bless the work of the missionaries
who have left home and friends
to spread the knowledge and love of you in other lands.

Dear Mother Mary,
bless all who are trying to bring Jesus to the people of the world who do not know him.

FOR MISSIONARIES

O Sacred Heart of Jesus Christ, look down on your missionaries, who for love of you and of the souls so precious to you, have gladly left their own country and the family they loved.
Help them to carry on your work of bringing the Church and its sacraments to every country, and of teaching all peoples.
Let not their hearts be torn with sorrow at having to send away the souls who are hungry for the Bread of Eternal life.
Comfort them in hardship and trouble.
Make them feel that you are with them in their loneliness.
Give them grace to persevere to the end in the life of suffering to which you have called them.
O Sacred Heart, for your own glory, remember your missionaries.

FOR ONE'S TEACHERS

Dear Lord Jesus, you have shown your love and trust for our teachers by calling them to work for what is dearer to you than your very life.
May every breath they draw, every word they say, be all for your greater honour and glory.

Remain in their hearts always and guide their thoughts, their words and their actions, so that they will always think and say and do what you yourself would think and say and do.
Dear Lord Jesus, you know that they want to gain each child for you.
May they be a safeguard and shield to all who are under their care.
Help them to teach solid devotion, that will protect their children in times of temptation.
Make them all you intended them to be when you called them to work in your vineyard.
Teach them how to teach well.
Help them to watch carefully and tenderly over the souls given to them.
Grant that through their silent influence, many of their children will realise what a wonderful thing it is to be your very own and will be willing to leave all and follow you when you call.
Make their school like the holy house of Nazareth, a place of faith and charity, of honour, work and prayer, of order and peace.
Grant your blessing to their work, so that when they stand in the brightness of your presence, they may say in the fullness of their joy, "Of those whom you have given me, I have not lost one." Amen.

FOR THOSE SEEKING THE FAITH

Open to your servants, O God, all the paths of faith, so that they may reach the safety and love of your Church.
Make known more fully to them the way of truth,

so that they may learn how to avoid the ways of error.
May they recognise the things that lead to salvation.
May they understand the treasures of life.
May they lay aside all that still remains with them of the things of darkness.
May they receive the brightness of the full light of Christ.
May the stains and sins of the world leave them completely, so that they may be worthily prepared for the holiness of baptism.
Christ Jesus, you who open all doors and make known the way of salvation, be pleased to love your servants who have come to the knowledge of your name and your love.
May they desire to follow you in their thoughts, you whom they have begun to confess with their mouths. Amen.

FOR FRIENDS IN PURGATORY

Good Jesus, whose loving heart was always troubled by the sorrows of others, look with pity on the souls of our loved friends in purgatory. You who "loved your own", hear my cry for mercy, and grant that those whom you called from our home in this world, may soon enjoy everlasting rest in the home of your love in heaven. Amen.

FOR THE SOULS IN PURGATORY

O Lord, because you are always most merciful and most generous with your gifts, look down upon the suffering souls in purgatory and heal them.

Because you have loved them from all eternity, be merciful and forgive their offences.
Cleanse them of their sins, and fulfil their burning desire to see you face to face in your glory.
May they soon enter into the happiness of the kingdom prepared for them, there to be united to you for ever and ever. Amen.
Eternal rest give unto them, O Lord, and let never-ending light shine upon them.
May the souls of all the faithful departed, through the mercy of God, rest in peace. Amen.

PRAYERS FOR ONESELF

FOR UNSELFISH LOVE

Lord make me an instrument of your peace;
where there is hatred, let me sow peace;
where there is injury, let me sow pardon;
where there is doubt, let me sow faith;
where there is despair, let me give hope;
where there is darkness, let me give light;
where there is sadness, let me give joy.
O Divine Master, grant that I may
not try to be comforted, but to comfort;
not try to be understood, but to understand;
not try to be loved, but to love.
Because it is in giving that we receive,
it is in forgiving that we are forgiven,
and it is in dying that we are born
into eternal life. Amen.
(St Francis of Assisi.)

FOR LOVE

Lord, you are all merciful,
take away my sins from me,
and give to my soul
the graces of your Holy Spirit.

Take away this heart of stone from me,
and give me a heart of flesh and blood,
a heart to love and adore you,
a heart which will delight in you,
love you and please you,
for the sake of Christ. Amen.
(St Ambrose.)

FOR LOVE TOWARDS OTHERS

Keep me, O God, from smallness of mind.
Let me be big in thought, in word and in action.
Let me be finished for ever
with fault-finding and self-love.
May I put away all pretending
and meet everyone face to face
without self-pity or deceit.
May I never be hasty in judging
and may I be always generous.
Let me take time for all things.
Make me grow calm, peaceful and gentle.
Teach me to put into action my good desires.
Teach me to be straightforward and fearless.
Grant that I may realise
that it is the little things of life
that make difficulties and divisions
and that in the big things of life we are one.
And, O Lord God, do not let me forget to be
kind.
My God, make us all of one mind in the
truth, and of one heart in love. Amen.

TEACH ME TO BE GENEROUS

Dearest Jesus, teach me to be generous.
Teach me to serve you as you deserve;
to give and not to count the cost;
to fight and not to think of wounds;
to work and look for no reward,
except that of knowing
that I am doing your holy will.

FOR MEEKNESS AND GENTLENESS

Teach me, my Lord, to be sweet and gentle
in all the actions of my life,
in disappointments,
in the thoughtlessness of others,
in the insincerity of those I trusted.
Let me forget myself,
that I may enjoy the happiness of others.
Let me always hide my little pains and heartaches,
that I may be the only one to suffer from them.
Teach me to profit from the suffering
that comes across my path.
Let me so use it
that it may soften me, not harden me,
that it may make me patient, not angry,
that it may make me willing to forgive,
not bitter or proud.
May no one be less good
for having come within my influence.
May no one be less pure, less true, less kind,
for having travelled with me
on our journey towards eternal life.
As I go from one work to another
let me whisper a word of love to you.
Let me live my life in the supernatural,
full of power for good,
and strong in my purpose of sanctity.
Amen.

FOR BROTHERLY LOVE

O Lord our God, I pray to you for myself and all my friends and neighbours. I offer you our hearts that they may be united in the strongest and most sincere brotherly love.

I pray that Jesus in the Blessed Sacrament may be the daily food of our souls. I pray that Jesus may be the centre of our love, just as he was for Mary and Joseph.

Finally, O Lord, may sin never disturb our union on earth ; and may we be all united in heaven with you and Mary and Joseph and all the saints. Amen.

PRAYER TO ASK GOD'S MERCY

Look down, O Lord, from your holy dwelling place, from heaven, your home. Look on this holy Victim, which our great High Priest, the Lord Jesus, offers up to you for the sins of the people, and do not be angry because of our many sins.

Behold, the voice of the blood of Jesus, our brother, cries to you from the cross. Listen to him, O Lord ! Be satisfied, O Lord ! Hear him, O Lord, and give us your grace. For your own sake, O my God, because your name is called on in prayer for this country and for your people, deal with us according to your great mercy. Amen.
(St Bernard and St Cajetan.)

THE SOUL'S OFFERING

I come to you, my Lord,
With tearful eyes and bruised and bleeding feet,
Torn by the world's hard ways and stony streets,
Its desert bleak and bare ;
Sore, wounded, and in bitter misery,

And heavy laden, save alone to you
Can I go anywhere?
Whene'er I turn from you, I lose the light
That guided me before through darkest night,
And blindly feel my way,
On the hard road of sinfulness and wrong,
Stumbling and falling as I go along,
With hope all taken away.
O lead me, Lord, unto your feet anew,
The feet that once for me were tired
and bleeding, too!

I come to you, O Lord,
An idle servant and with empty hands,
The prodigal from distant foreign lands,
Where all my store was spent.
Nothing have I to say, but silent wait
Before the pillars of your mercy-gate.
With drooping head and bent,
Until the time when you will travel by
And seeing all my weakness, cast your eye
On one so worn and weak,
One who has not the wedding garment on
And lost the light that once upon him shone,
And who can nothing speak,
Save that one cry that always heard will be,
"I am a sinner, Lord, be merciful to me."

I come to you, my Lord,
And yet I have no gift that I can bring
Such as may give you joy, O thorn-crowned king:
None save myself alone
And my tired heart that wandered aimlessly,
Seeking for joys upon the world's wild sea,

For peace, yet finding none.
Will you accept this worthless offering?
Alas! dear Lord, 'tis all I have to bring—
How poor and yet my all!
And, knowing this, you will not turn away
But bend your ear to listen while I pray,
And on your name I call.
Gather up once more life's broken strands,
And bless your child once more
with your dear wounded hands.

PRAYER FOR GRACE TO DO GOD'S WILL

Take, O Lord, all my freedom.
Take my memory, my mind and my whole will.
You have given me all I have or own.
I give all back to you, and offer myself completely to you,
so that I may follow your holy will.
Give me your love and your grace,
and then I shall be rich enough and will ask for nothing more. Amen.

THE LOWEST PLACE

Give me the lowest place; not that I dare
Ask for that lowest place, had you not died
    That I might live and share
    Your glory by your side.

Give me that lowest place; or if for me
That lowest place too high, make one more low
    Where I may sit and see
    My God, and love you so.

A LITANY OF INVOCATIONS

O God, who is, have pity on me who am not,
for through you alone I live and move and am.
Our Father, who art in heaven, thy kingdom come,
reign in my heart now and for ever.

O Lord Jesus Christ,
who died on the cross for all poor sinners
have mercy on my sinful soul.

Holy Ghost, in whom we cry, "Father!"
give me grace to say, "Lord Jesus", with full faith and love.

Holy Mary, Mother of God,
look on me with loving pity,
turn to your divine Son,
and tell him that I love you.

St Joseph, who died in the loving arms
of Jesus and Mary,
help me with your prayers,
so that my death may in some way be like yours.

St Peter, chief pastor under the Good Shepherd,
keep me safe within the fold of the Church.

St Paul, help me to escape the punishment
that falls on those who do not love Jesus.

St John, pray for me,
that I also may claim the title
of the disciple whom Jesus loved,
because he is pleased to allow me
a closer union with him in Holy Communion than
you had, leaning upon his breast.

St Thomas, obtain for me the grace to say,
with some poor share of your burning faith:
"My Lord and my God!"
especially when I kneel before the tabernacle.

St Augustine, remind me to pray for my mother,
as you prayed for St Monica at the altar,
in obedience to her last wishes.

St Thomas Aquinas, obtain for me some share
in your delight
in thinking on the truths of our faith,
and some share in the love which filled your heart
when you wrote about the Blessed Sacrament.

St Aloysius, pray that at Holy Communion
I may have some of the joyful love and faith
which filled your innocent heart
when you received your first Communion.

St Teresa, obtain for me
some of your loving trust in the patronage of
St Joseph.

Blessed Peter Favre, obtain for me
some little part of your habit of ejaculatory prayer.

St Margaret Mary, pray that I may love with my
whole heart
the Sacred Heart of Jesus, so loving and so little
loved.

O Lamb of God,
who takes away the sins of the world,
spare us, hear us kindly and have mercy on us,
O Lord God.

A PRAYER OF YOUTH

Make of our youth, O God, a holy thing,
Let it not languish, die and naught avail.
Tend it, we pray you, in its blossoming,
Give it the beauty that can never fail.

Let us not pass in dreams of fantasy
The rich young morning, heeding not your call,
Then at cold dusk, to waken suddenly
And, terror-stricken, watch the swift night fall.

You who gave our manhood dignity,
Set our young hearts with ardour all aflame,
Make us true soldiers of your chivalry,
Loving your hallowed standard and your name.

Let us not waste your splendid gift, O King,
Or barter it for all the world's poor price,
Make of our youth, O God, a holy thing,
Make of our hearts, O Lord, your sacrifice.

(Benen.)

BEFORE READING OR STUDY

Give me grace, O merciful God,
to desire strongly all that is pleasing to you,
to examine it carefully,
to accept it truthfully,
and to perform it perfectly,
for the praise and glory of your name.
Amen.

I CANNOT PRAY

Ah, dearest Lord, I cannot pray,
My fancy is not free;
Disorderly distractions come
And force my thoughts from thee.

This world that looks so dull all day,
Glows bright on me at prayer,
And plans that ask no thought but then,
Wake up and find me there.

Old voices murmur in my ear,
New hopes start into life,
And past and future gaily blend,
In one absorbing strife.

I cannot pray, yet Lord, you know
The pain it is for me
To have my vainly struggling thoughts,
Thus torn away from thee.

Sweet Jesus, teach me how to prize,
These tedious hours when I,
Foolish and mute, before your face
In helpless worship lie.

My Saviour, why should I complain,
And why fear aught but sin?
Distractions are but outward things,
Your peace dwells far within.

These surface troubles come and go
Like rufflings of the sea,
The deeper depth is out of reach
To all, my God, but thee.

MAY MY LIFE BE ALL FOR THEE

Take my life and let it be,
Offered up, O Lord, to thee.
Take my moments and my days,
Let them flow in endless praise.

Take my voice and let it sing,
Always, only for my King.
Take my lips and let them be
Filled with messages from thee.

Take my intellect and use,
Every power as thou shalt choose.
Take my heart, it is thine own,
Let it be thy royal throne.

Take my love, my Lord, I pour
At thy feet its treasure store,
Take myself and I will be,
Ever, only, all for thee.

KEEP ME FROM SIN

Take my body, Jesus,
    Eyes and ears and tongue,
Never let them, Jesus,
    Help to do thee wrong.

Take my heart and fill it
    Full of love for thee;
All I have I give thee,
    Give thyself to me.

ACTS OF LOVE AND THE OTHER VIRTUES

Make my heart your home of love, dear Jesus, in which you love to live, and from which you call others to your love. Make me love every moment of my life, till I perfectly fulfil the desire of your love.

Your will, not mine be done.
My God, teach me.
Help me to help others.
I love you.
I trust you and leave all to you.
I hope in you.

I am sorry for all my sins.
I thank you.
I love you and praise you.
I ask you for all I need.
I humble myself before you.
I long for you.
Now, and at the hour of my death. Amen.

REMEMBRANCE FOR EVERY DAY

The will of God be done by us,
The law of God be kept by us,
Our evil will controlled by us,
Repentance made in time by us,
Christ's passion understood by us,
All sinful crimes refused by us,
Our end remembered well by us,
And death be blessed found by us,
With angel's music heard by us,
And God's high praises sung by us,
For ever and for ever. Amen.

PRAYER FOR THE LOVE OF GOD AND OF OUR NEIGHBOUR

O my God, you are charity and love itself,
make charity and love grow perfect in me,
so that your love may burn up all my self-love.

My only treasure,
all my glory,
make me love you more than any created thing,
so that I may love myself in you
and love my neighbour and help him in his difficulties.

Apart from you
may I never love anything that exists,
and may I use all things to go to you,
and for nothing else.

I am glad and will be glad because of the perfect love you have for yourself,
in the endless love that the angels and saints have for you in heaven.

I am glad because your holy servants on earth
who know you by the light of faith,
know that you alone are their highest good,
and the centre of their love.

I desire that all sinners in this world
should love you in this way,
and with your grace,
I will help them to do so. Amen.
(St Teresa.)

PRAYERS BEFORE COMMUNION

PRAYER FOR HELP

O my God, help me to make a good Communion.
Mary, my dearest Mother, pray to Jesus for me.
All you holy angels and saints, pray for me.
My Angel Guardian, lead me to the altar of God.

ACT OF FAITH

O God, because you have said it,
I believe that I shall receive the sacred body of Jesus Christ to eat,
and his precious blood to drink.
My God, I believe this with all my heart.

HUMILITY

My God, I confess that I am a poor sinner;
I am not worthy
to receive the body and blood of Jesus.
Lord I am not worthy that you should enter under my roof;
say but the word, and my soul shall be healed.

SORROW

My God, I detest all the sins of my life.
I am sorry for them because they have offended you, my God,
who art so good.
I resolve never, never to commit sin any more.
My good God, pity me, have mercy on me,
forgive me. Amen.

ADORATION

O Jesus, great God,
present on the altar,
I bow down before you, I adore you.

LOVE AND DESIRE

Sweet Jesus, I love you.
I desire with all my heart to receive you.
Most sweet Jesus, come into my poor soul,
and give me your flesh to eat and your blood to drink.
Give me your whole self,
body, blood, soul and divinity,
that I may live for ever with you. Amen.

PRAYER FOR ALL VIRTUES

I believe in you, Lord, may I believe more firmly.
I hope in you, Lord, may I hope more surely.
I love you, Lord, may I love you more and more.
I repent of my sins, may my sorrow always grow deeper.

I adore you because you made me from nothing.
I desire you because you made me for yourself.
I praise you because everything good in my life comes from you.
I call on you for help, because you are my merciful protector.

Guide me by your wisdom.
Keep me in your grace.
Comfort me in your mercy.
Protect me by your power.

I offer you my thoughts, that they may be directed towards you.
I offer you my words, that they may be spoken for your glory.
I offer you my actions, that I may perform them according to your will.
I offer you my trials and sufferings, that I may accept them for your sake.

I desire whatever you desire;
I desire it because you desire it,
in so far as you desire it,
and as long as you desire it.

I beg of you, Lord, to clear my mind with the light of your truth,
and to make my will burn with love.
I pray you to make my heart clean and my soul holy.

May I turn away from sins of the past.
May I overcome the temptations of the future.
May I correct my sinful desires.
May I cause all the virtues I need to grow in my soul.

O good God, grant that I may love your goodness,
that I may hate my sinfulness,
that I may help my neighbour
and that I may set small value on the riches and pleasures of this world.

May I be careful to obey my superiors,
to help those in my care,
to give good advice to my friends,
and to be kind to my enemies.

May I overcome the desire for sinful pleasure by self-denial.
May I overcome the desire for wealth by generosity.
May I overcome my anger by patience,
and may I overcome my spiritual laziness by whole-hearted love and service.

Make me prudent in instructing others.
Make me brave in times of danger.
Make me patient in times of trial
and make me humble and thankful when things go well.

Grant, Lord, that I may pray well;
that I may eat and drink reasonably;
that I may fulfil my duty carefully,
and that I may carry out my good intentions
firmly and faithfully.

May I take care to be clean in soul,
to be modest in body,
to be a good example in conversation
and to live my life according to your law.

May I carefully be on the look out for my sinful inclinations so that I may overcome them.
May I keep watch for your graces so that I may make use of them.
May I keep your law before my eyes so that I may follow it.
May I remember always my eternal salvation,
so that I may work for it.

May I learn from you how useless and empty are the things of this world,
and how splendid are the things of God.
May I remember always from your teaching how short this life is,
and how long and lasting is the life of heaven.

Grant that I may be always ready for death,
that I may fear your judgment,
that I may escape hell and that I may reach heaven.
Amen.
(Pope Clement XI.)

PRAYERS AFTER COMMUNION

ACT OF FAITH

O Jesus, I believe
that I have received your flesh to eat and your blood to drink,
because you have said it and your word is true.

ADORATION

O Jesus, my God, and my Creator,
I adore you,
because from your hands I came,
and with you I am to be happy for ever.

HUMILITY

O Jesus, I am but dust and ashes,
and yet you have come to me that my poor heart may speak to you.

LOVE

Sweet Jesus, I love you with all my heart.
You know that I love you,
and that I wish to love you daily more and more.

THANKSGIVING

My good Jesus, I thank you with all my heart.
How good, how kind you are to me, sweet Jesus.
Blessed be Jesus in the most holy sacrament of the altar.

OFFERING

O Jesus, receive my poor offering.
Jesus, you have given yourself to me,
now let me give myself to you.
I give you my *body*, that it may be chaste and pure.
I give you my *soul,* that it may be free from sin.
I give you my *heart,* that it may always love you.
I give you every *breath* that I shall breathe,
and especially my last;
I give you *myself* in life and in death,
that I may be yours for ever and ever.

PRAYER FOR ONESELF

O Jesus, wash away my sins with your precious blood.
O Jesus, the struggle against temptation is not yet finished.
My Jesus, when temptation comes near me,
make me strong against it.
In the moment of temptation
may I always say, "Jesus, mercy! Mary, help!"
O Jesus, may I lead a good life,
may I die a happy death.
May I receive you before I die.
May I say when I am dying,
"Jesus, Mary and Joseph, I give you my heart and my soul."

PRAYER FOR OTHERS

O Jesus, have mercy on your holy Church, take care of it.
O Jesus, have pity on poor sinners and save them from hell.

O Jesus, bless my father, my mother, my brothers and sisters,
and all I ought to pray for,
as your kind heart knows how to bless them.
O Jesus, have pity on the souls in purgatory,
and give them eternal rest.
My Jesus, grant pardon and mercy,
through the merits of your sacred wounds.
Eternal Father,
I offer you the wounds of our Lord Jesus Christ
to heal those of our souls.
Sacred Heart of Jesus, I trust in you.
Sweet Heart of Mary, be my salvation.

BEFORE LEAVING THE CHURCH

Sweet Jesus, I am going away for a time,
but I trust not without you.
You are with me by your grace.
I will never leave you by mortal sin.
I do not fear to do so,
though I am so weak,
because I have such hopes in you.
Give me grace to persevere. Amen.

Additional Prayers after Communion

ACT OF FAITH

Who comes?
The Word made man for me,
the Lord who died for me,
the Lord made food for me,
he comes.

To whom does he come?

To one redeemed by him,
to one united to him,
to one who belongs to him,
he comes.

Why does he come?

To reign upon his throne,
to reign supreme alone,
to make me all his own,
he comes.

AN OFFERING

O my God, whose love cannot be measured,
it is your love which has made you come to me.
It is my hope which has made me receive you.
I give you my body as a temple,
my will as a sacrifice,
my heart as an altar,
and my whole soul as a dwelling place.

O innocent Lamb of God, O boundless Mercy,
let me live in your body,
shelter me in your heart,
hide me in your wounds,
wash me in your blood,
make me burn with love
in the sweet fire of your friendship,
strengthen me with your love,
give me new life by your death.
O Lord, O most noble and humble Lord,
through the merits of your Sacred Heart,
grant that I may please you in all things. Amen.

TRUST IN GOD'S MERCY

O Lord, my God,
I am not worthy that you should come into my soul;
but because according to your loving kindness, it is your will to dwell in me,
I am glad you have come to me.

You ask me to open the gates of my soul,
which you alone have made,
so that you may come in with your usual loving kindness,
to give light to my darkened mind.

I believe that you will do this,
for you did not refuse Mary Magdalen when she came to you in tears.
Nor did you refuse to forgive the publican who was sorry for his sins,
or the good thief who prayed to be received into your kingdom.
But you counted among your friends all those who came to you in sorrow,
O God,
who alone are blessed, always, now, and to everlasting ages. Amen.

(St John Chrysostom.)

SOUL OF MY SAVIOUR

Soul of my Saviour, sanctify my breast,
Body of Christ, be thou my saving guest,
Blood of my Saviour, bathe me in thy tide,
Wash me, ye waters, gushing from his side.

Strength and protection may his passion be,
O blessed Jesus, hear and answer me.
Deep in thy wounds, Lord, hide and shelter me
So shall I never, never part from thee.

Guard and defend me from the foe malign;
In death's drear moments, make me wholly thine;
Call me, and bid me come to thee on high,
Where I may praise thee with thy saints for aye.

PRAYER OF LOVE AND PETITION

I have found him whom my soul loves;
I hold him and will not let him go.

I embrace you, O my Jesus, and am glad with the full joy of my love.
I possess you, the treasure of my heart, in whom I possess all things.
I beg of you, let my soul feel the power of your presence;
let it taste how sweet you are, O my Lord;
let it be taken prisoner by your love,
so that it may seek no one else but you,
nor love anyone else except for your sake.

You are my king,
forget not my trouble and my need.

You are my judge,
spare me and be merciful to me.

You are the doctor of my soul,
heal my weakness.

You are the spouse of my soul,
may I be united to you for evermore.

You are my leader and defender,
place me by your side,
and then I shall not care whose hands are lifted against me.

You have offered yourself as a victim for me,
and I will offer to you a sacrifice of praise.

You are my Saviour,
save my soul from the power of hell and keep me always.

You are my God and my all
—for what have I in heaven but you,
and besides you, what do I desire upon earth?
You, O my God, are the God of my heart,
and my choice for ever. Amen.

THE ORDER OF MASS

The Introductory Rites

The priest and the ministers go to the altar and the entrance song is sung. When the entrance song is ended the priest and the faithful cross themselves.

Celebrant. In the name of the Father, and of the Son, and of the Holy Spirit.
People. **Amen.**
C. The Lord be with you.
P. **And also with you.**

Other forms of greeting

2. *C.* The grace of our Lord Jesus Christ and the love of God and the fellowship of the Holy Spirit be with you all.
   P. **And also with you.**

or

3. *C.* The grace and peace of God our Father and the Lord Jesus Christ be with you.
   P. **Blessed be God, the Father of our Lord Jesus Christ.**

or

   P. **And also with you.**

The Penitential Rite

C. My brothers and sisters,* to prepare ourselves to celebrate the sacred mysteries, let us call to mind our sins.

After a brief silence all say:

All. **I confess to almighty God,**
and to you, my brothers and sisters,
that I have sinned through my own fault
(*All strike their breast*)

---

* Other words, such as "my dear people, friends, dearly beloved, brethren," may be used here and in similar places in the liturgy.

in my thoughts and in my words,
in what I have done,
and in what I have failed to do;
and I ask blessed Mary, ever virgin,
all the angels and saints,
and you, my brothers and sisters,
to pray for me to the Lord our God.

The priest says the absolution

Other forms of the Penitential Rite

2. *C.* My brothers and sisters, to prepare ourselves to celebrate the sacred mysteries, let us call to mind our sins:

After a brief silence, the celebrant says:

C. Lord, we have sinned against you:
Lord, have mercy.
P. **Lord, have mercy.**
C. Lord, show us your mercy and love.
P. **And grant us your salvation.**

The priest says the absolution.

or

3. *C.* My brothers and sisters, to prepare ourselves to celebrate the sacred mysteries, let us call to mind our sins.

After a brief silence, the celebrant makes the following or other invocations with "Lord have mercy".

C. You were sent to heal the contrite:
Lord, have mercy.
P. **Lord, have mercy.**
C. You came to call sinners:
Christ, have mercy.
P. **Christ, have mercy.**
C. You plead for us at the right hand of the Father:
Lord, have mercy.
P. **Lord, have mercy.**

The priest says the absolution.

The absolution

C. May almighty God have mercy on us,
forgive us our sins,
and bring us to everlasting life.

P. **Amen.**

The following is not said if it has already been incorporated in the penitential rite

C. Lord, have mercy.
P. **Lord, have mercy.**
C. Christ, have mercy.
P. **Christ, have mercy.**
C. Lord, have mercy.
P. **Lord, have mercy.**

The Gloria

(When it is prescribed. This may be said or sung.)

Glory to God in the highest,
and peace to his people on earth.

Lord God, heavenly King,
almighty God and Father,
we worship you, we give you thanks,
we praise you for your glory.

Lord Jesus Christ, only Son of the Father,
Lord God, Lamb of God,
you take away the sin of the world:
have mercy on us;
you are seated at the right hand of the Father:
receive our prayer.

For you alone are the Holy One,
you alone are the Lord,
you alone are the Most High,
Jesus Christ,
with the Holy Spirit,
in the glory of God the Father. Amen.

THE LITURGY OF THE WORLD

C. Let us pray.

All pray silently with the priest for a while. Then the priest says the opening prayer (collect), to which the people respond:

P. **Amen.**

THE LITURGY OF THE WORD

First Reading

At the end of the first reading:

Reader. This is the Word of the Lord.
All. **Thanks be to God.**

Responsorial Psalm

The Cantor sings or recites the psalm, and the people make ths response (see Proper of the Mass for the Day).

Second Reading

At the end of the Second Reading:

Reader. This is the Word of the Lord.
All. **Thanks be to God.**

Alleluia or Acclamation

The Alleluia or another chant follows (see Proper of the Mass forth Day). The people sing or say this chant.

The Gospel

C. The Lord be with you.
P. **And also with you.**
C. A reading from the holy gospel according to N.
P. **Glory to you, Lord.**

At the end of the Gospel:

C. This is the gospel of the Lord.
P. **Praise to you, Lord Jesus Christ.**

Homily

Creed

We believe in one God,
the Father, the Almighty,
maker of heaven and earth,
of all that is, seen and unseen.

We believe in one Lord, Jesus Christ,
the only Son of God,
eternally begotten of the Father,
God from God, Light from Light,
true God from true God,
begotten, not made,
of one Being with the Father,
Through him all things were made.
For us men and for our salvation
he came down from heaven:
(*all bow during these three lines*)
by the power of the Holy Spirit
he became incarnate from the Virgin Mary and was made man.
For our sake he was crucified under Pontius Pilate;
he suffered death and was buried.
On the third day he rose again
in accordance with the Scriptures;
he ascended into heaven
and is seated at the right hand of the Father.
He will come again in glory to judge the living and the dead, and his kingdom will have no end.

We believe in the Holy Spirit, the Lord, the giver of life, who proceeds from the Father and the Son.
With the Father and the Son he is worshipped and glorified.
He has spoken through the Prophets.
We believe in one holy Catholic and apostolic Church.
We acknowledge one baptism for the forgiveness of sins.
We look for the resurrection of the dead,
and the life of the world to come. Amen.

THE OFFERING

Then follows

The prayer of the faithful

(*The prayer begins with an invitation, followed by a series of petitions to which the people answer* **Lord, graciously hear us,** *and concludes with a prayer by the celebrant to which the people answer* **Amen.**)

'THE LITURGY OF THE EUCHARIST

The offering

During the offertory, the people may sing an offertory song, while the priest says the following quietly. If no song is sung then the people may make the responses given here to the prayer of offering.

C. Blessed are you, Lord, God of all creation.
Through your goodness we have this bread to offer,
which earth has given and human hands have made.
It will become for us the bread of life.

P. **Blessed be God for ever.**

C. By the mystery of this water and wine
may we come to share in the divinity of Christ,
who humbled himself to share in our humanity.

Blessed are you, Lord, God of all creation.
Through your goodness we have this wine to offer,
fruit of the vine and work of human hands.
It will become our spiritual drink.

P. **Blessed be God for ever.**

C. Lord God, we ask you to receive us
and be pleased with the sacrifice we offer you
with humble and contrite hearts.

The priest washes his hands, saying quietly:

C. Lord, wash away my iniquity;
cleanse me from my sin.

Pray, brethren, that our sacrifice
may be acceptable to God, the almighty Father.

P. **May the Lord accept the sacrifice at your hands**
for the praise and glory of his name,
for our good, and the good of all his Church.

The priest says or sings the prayer over the gifts.

P. **Amen.**

The Eucharistic Prayer

C. The Lord be with you.
P. **And also with you.**
C. Lift up your hearts.
P. **We lift them up to the Lord.**
C. Let us give thanks to the Lord our God.
P. **It is right to give him thanks and praise.**

The Preface

The celebrant continues alone. At the end of the Preface:

All. **Holy, holy, holy Lord, God of power and might,**
heaven and earth are full of your glory.
Hosanna in the highest.
Blessed is he who comes in the name of the Lord.
Hosanna in the highest.

Eucharistic Prayer I

(*The passages within the brackets may be omitted if the celebrant wishes.*)

The celebrant continues:

We come to you, Father,
with praise and thanksgiving,
through Jesus Christ your Son.
Through him we ask you to accept and bless
these gifts we offer you in sacrifice.

For the Church

We offer them for your holy catholic Church,
watch over it, Lord, and guide it;

grant it peace and unity throughout the world.
We offer them for N. our Pope,
for N. our bishop,
and for all who hold and teach the catholic faith
that comes to us from the apostles.

Remember, Lord, your people,
especially those for whom we now pray, N. and N.
Remember all of us gathered here before you.
You know how firmly we believe in you
and dedicate ourselves to you.
We offer you this sacrifice of praise
for ourselves and those who are dear to us.
We pray to you, our living and true God,
for our well-being and redemption.

To honour the saints

In union with the whole Church
we honour Mary,
the ever-virgin mother of Jesus Christ our Lord and God.
We honour Joseph, her husband,
the apostles and martyrs
Peter and Paul, Andrew,
(James, John, Thomas,
James, Philip,
Bartholomew, Matthew, Simon and Jude;
we honour Linus, Cletus, Clement, Sixtus,
Cornelius, Cyprian, Lawrence, Chrysogonus,
John and Paul, Cosmas and Damian)
and all the saints.
May their merits and prayers
gain us your constant help and protection.
(Through Christ our Lord. Amen.)

For general needs

Father, accept this offering
from your whole family.
Grant us your peace in this life,
save us from final damnation,

and count us among those you have chosen.
(Through Christ our Lord. Amen.)

For acceptance

Bless and approve our offering;
make it acceptable to you,
an offering in spirit and in truth.
Let it become for us
the body and blood of Jesus Christ,
your only Son, our Lord.

The Lord's supper

The day before he suffered
he took bread in his sacred hands
and looking up to heaven,
to you, his almighty Father,
he gave you thanks and praise.
He broke the bread,
gave it to his disciples, and said:

Take this, all of you, and eat it:
this is my body which will be given up for you.

When supper was ended,
he took the cup.
Again he gave you thanks and praise,
gave the cup to his disciples, and said:

Take this, all of you, and drink from it:
this is the cup of my blood,
the blood of the new and everlasting covenant.
It will be shed for you and for all men
so that sins may be forgiven.
Do this in memory of me.

C. Let us proclaim the mystery of faith:

Memorial acclamation of the people

P. **1. Christ has died,**
Christ is risen,
Christ will come again.

Alternative acclamations

P. **2. Dying you destroyed our death,**
rising you restored our life.
Lord Jesus, come in glory.

3. When we eat this bread and drink this cup,
we proclaim your death, Lord Jesus,
until you come in glory.

4. Lord, by your cross and resurrection
you have set us free.
You are the Saviour of the world.

Memorial and offering

Father, we celebrate the memory of Christ, your Son.
We, your people and your ministers,
recall his passion,
his resurrection from the dead,
and his ascension into glory;
and from the many gifts you have given us
we offer to you, God of glory and majesty,
this holy and perfect sacrifice:
the bread of life
and the cup of eternal salvation.

Look with favour on these offerings
and accept them as once you accepted
the gifts of your servant Abel,
the sacrifice of Abraham, our father in faith,
and the bread and wine offered by your priest Melchisedech.

Almighty God,
we pray that your angel may take this sacrifice
to your altar in heaven.
Then, as we receive from this altar
the sacred body and blood of your Son,
let us be filled with every grace and blessing.
(Through Christ our Lord. Amen.)

For the dead

Remember, Lord, those who have died
and have gone before us marked with the sign of faith,
especially those for whom we now pray, N. and N.
May these, and all who sleep in Christ,
find in your presence
light, happiness, and peace.
(Through Christ our Lord. Amen.)

For us sinners

For ourselves, too, we ask
some share in the fellowship of your apostles and martyrs,
with John the Baptist, Stephen, Matthias, Barnabas,
(Ignatius, Alexander, Marcellinus, Peter,
Felicity, Perpetua, Agatha, Lucy,
Agnes, Cecilia, Anastasia)
and all the saints.
Though we are sinners,
we trust in your mercy and love.
Do not consider what we truly deserve,
but grant us your forgiveness.

Through Christ our Lord
you give us all these gifts.
You fill them with life and goodness,
you bless them and make them holy.

Concluding doxology

Through him,
with him,
in him,
in the unity of the Holy Spirit,
all glory and honour is yours,
almighty Father,
for ever and ever.

P. **Amen.**

Continue on p. 196.

Eucharistic Prayer II

Praise to the Father

C. Father, it is our duty and our salvation,
always and everywhere
to give you thanks
through your beloved Son, Jesus Christ.
He is the Word through whom you made the universe,
the Saviour you sent to redeem us.
By the power of the Holy Spirit
he took flesh and was born of the Virgin Mary.
For our sake he opened his arms on the cross;
he put an end to death
and revealed the resurrection.
In this he fulfilled your will
and won for you a holy people.
And so we join the angels and the saints
in proclaiming your glory
as we sing (say):

First acclamation of the people

All. **Holy, holy, holy . . .**

Invocation of the Holy Spirit

C. Lord, you are holy indeed,
the fountain of all holiness.
Let your Spirit come upon these gifts to make them holy,
so that they may become for us
the body and blood of our Lord, Jesus Christ.

The Lord's supper

Before he was given up to death,
a death he freely accepted,
he took bread and gave you thanks.
He broke the bread,
gave it to his disciples, and said:

Take this, all of you, and eat it:
this is my body which will be given up for you.

When supper was ended, he took the cup.
Again he gave you thanks and praise,
gave the cup to his disciples, and said:

Take this, all of you, and drink from it:
this is the cup of my blood,
the blood of the new and everlasting covenant.
It will be shed for you and for all men
so that sins may be forgiven.
Do this in memory of me.

C. Let us proclaim the mystery of faith:

Memorial acclamation of the people

P. **1. Christ has died,**
Christ is risen,
Christ will come again.

Alternative acclamations

P. **2. Dying you destroyed our death,**
rising you restored our life.
Lord Jesus, come in glory.

3. When we eat this bread and drink this cup,
we proclaim your death, Lord Jesus,
until you come in glory.

4. Lord, by your cross and resurrection
you have set us free.
You are the Saviour of the world.

EUCHARISTIC PRAYER II

The memorial prayer

C. In memory of his death and resurrection,
we offer you, Father, this life-giving bread,
this saving cup.
We thank you for counting us worthy
to stand in your presence and serve you.

Invocation of the Holy Spirit

May all of us who share in the body and blood of Christ
be brought together in unity by the Holy Spirit.

Intercessions for the Church

Lord, remember your Church throughout the world;
make us grow in love,
together with N. our Pope,
N. our bishop, and all the clergy.

(In Masses for the Dead the following may be added:

Remember N., whom you have called from this life.
In baptism he [she] died with Christ:
may he [she] also share his resurrection.)

For the dead

Remember our brothers and sisters
who have gone to their rest
in the hope of rising again;
bring them and all the departed
into the light of your presence.

In communion with the Saints

Have mercy on us all;
make us worthy to share eternal life
with Mary, the virgin mother of God,
with the apostles,
and with all the saints who have done your will throughout the ages.
May we praise you in union with them,
and give you glory
through your Son, Jesus Christ.

Concluding doxology

Through him,
with him,
in him,
in the unity of the Holy Spirit,
all glory and honour is yours,
almighty Father,
for ever and ever.

P. **Amen.**

Continue on p. 616.

Eucharistic Prayer III

Praise to the Father

C. Father, you are holy indeed,
and all creation rightly gives you praise.
All life, all holiness comes from you
through your Son, Jesus Christ our Lord,
by the working of the Holy Spirit.
From age to age you gather a people to yourself,
so that from east to west
a perfect offering may be made
to the glory of your name.

Invocation of the Holy Spirit

And so, Father, we bring you these gifts.
We ask you to make them holy by the power of your Spirit,
that they may become the body and blood
of your Son, our Lord Jesus Christ,
at whose command we celebrate this eucharist.

The Lord's supper

On the night he was betrayed,
he took bread and gave you thanks and praise.
He broke the bread, gave it to his disciples, and said:

Take this, all of you, and eat it:
this is my body which will be given up for you.

When supper was ended, he took the cup.
Again he gave you thanks and praise,
gave the cup to his disciples, and said:

Take this, all of you, and drink from it:
this is the cup of my blood,
the blood of the new and everlasting covenant.
It will be shed for you and for all men
so that sins may be forgiven.
Do this in memory of me.

C. Let us proclaim the mystery of faith:

Memorial acclamation of the people

P. **1. Christ has died,**
Christ is risen,
Christ will come again.

Alternative acclamations

P. **2. Dying you destroyed our death,**
rising you restored our life.
Lord Jesus, come in glory.

3. When we eat this bread and drink this cup,
we proclaim your death, Lord Jesus,
until you come in glory.

4. Lord by your cross and resurrection
you have set us free.
You are the Saviour of the world.

The memorial prayer

C. Father, calling to mind the death your Son endured for our salvation,
his glorious resurrection and ascension into heaven,
and ready to greet him when he comes again,

we offer you in thanksgiving this holy and living sacrifice.

Look with favour on your Church's offering,
and see the Victim whose death has reconciled us to yourself.

Invocation of the Holy Spirit

Grant that we, who are nourished by his body and blood,
may be filled with his Holy Spirit,
and become one body, one spirit in Christ.

May he make us an everlasting gift to you
and enable us to share in the inheritance of your saints,
with Mary, the virgin Mother of God;
with the apostles, the martyrs,
(Saint N.—the patron saint or saint of the day) and all your saints,
on whose constant intercession we rely for help.

For the Church

Lord, may this sacrifice, which has made our peace with you,
advance the peace and salvation of all the world.
Strengthen in faith and love your pilgrim Church on earth;
your servant, Pope N., our bishop N., and all the bishops,
with the clergy and the entire people your Son has gained for you.
Father, hear the prayers of the family you have gathered here before you.
In mercy and love unite all your children
wherever they may be.

For the dead

Welcome into your kingdom our departed brothers and sisters,

and all who have left this world in your friendship.
We hope to enjoy for ever the vision of your glory,
through Christ our Lord, from whom all good things come.

Concluding doxology

Through him,
with him,
in him,
in the unity of the Holy Spirit,
all glory and honour is yours,
almighty Father,
for ever and ever.

P. **Amen.**

Continue on p. 616.

Eucharistic Prayer IV

Preface

C. Father in heaven, it is right that we should give you thanks and glory:
you alone are God, living and true.
Through all eternity you live in unapproachable light.
Source of life and goodness, you have created all things,
to fill your creatures with every blessing
and lead all men to the joyful vision of your light.
Countless hosts of angels stand before you to do your will;
they look upon your splendour
and praise you, night and day.
United with them, and in the name of every creature under heaven,
we too praise your glory as we sing (say):

First acclamation of the people

P. **Holy, holy, holy . . .**

Praise to the Father

C. Father, we acknowledge your greatness:
all your actions show your wisdom and love.
You formed man in your own likeness
and set him over the whole world
to serve you, his creator,
and to rule over all creatures.
Even when he disobeyed you and lost your friendship
you did not abandon him to the power of death,
but helped all men to seek and find you.
Again and again you offered a covenant to man,
and through the prophets taught him to hope for salvation.
Father, you so loved the world
that in the fullness of time you sent your only Son to be our Saviour.
He was conceived through the power of the Holy Spirit, and born of the Virgin Mary,
a man like us in all things but sin.
To the poor he proclaimed the good news of salvation,
to prisoners, freedom,
and to those in sorrow, joy.
In fulfilment of your will
he gave himself up to death;
but by rising from the dead,
he destroyed death and restored life.
And that we might live no longer for ourselves but for him,
he sent the Holy Spirit from you, Father,
as his first gift to those who believe,
to complete his work on earth
and bring us the fullness of grace.

Invocation of the Holy Spirit

Father, may this Holy Spirit sanctify these offerings.
Let them become the body and blood of Jesus Christ our Lord
as we celebrate the great mystery
which he left us as an everlasting covenant.

EUCHARISTIC PRAYER IV

The Lord's supper

He always loved those who were his own in the world.
When the time came for him to be glorified by you, his heavenly Father,
he showed the depth of his love.
While they were at supper,
he took bread, said the blessing, broke the bread
and gave it to his disciples, saying:

Take this, all of you, and eat it:
this is my body which will be given up for you.

In the same way, he took the cup, filled with wine.
He gave you thanks, and giving the cup to his disciples, said:

Take this all of you, and drink from it:
this is the cup of my blood,
the blood of the new and everlasting covenant.
It will be shed for you and for all men
so that sins may be forgiven.
Do this in memory of me.

Let us proclaim the mystery of faith:

Memorial acclamation of the people

P. **1. Christ has died,**
Christ is risen,
Christ will come again.

Alternative acclamations

P. **2. Dying you destroyed our death,**
rising you restored our life.
Lord Jesus, come in glory.

3. When we eat this bread and drink this cup,
we proclaim your death, Lord Jesus,
until you come in glory.

4. Lord, by your cross and resurrection you have set us free. You are the Saviour of the world.

The memorial prayer

C. Father, we now celebrate this memorial of our redemption.
We recall Christ's death, his descent among the dead, his resurrection, and his ascension to your right hand;
and, looking forward to his coming in glory, we offer you his body and blood,
the acceptable sacrifice which brings salvation to the whole world.

Lord, look upon this sacrifice which you have given to your Church:
and by your Holy Spirit, gather all who share this * bread and wine *
into the one body of Christ, a living sacrifice of praise.

Intercessions: for the Church

Lord, remember those for whom we offer this sacrifice,
especially N. our Pope,
N. our bishop, and bishops and clergy everywhere.
Remember those who take part in this offering,
those here present and all your people,
and all who seek you with a sincere heart.

For the dead

Remember those who have died in the peace of Christ
and all the dead whose faith is known to you alone.

---

* or: one bread and one cup

In communion with the saints

Father, in your mercy grant also to us, your children,
to enter into our heavenly inheritance
in the company of the Virgin Mary, the Mother of God,
and your apostles and saints.
Then, in your kingdom, freed from the corruption of sin and death,
we shall sing your glory with every creature through Christ our Lord,
through whom you give us everything that is good.

Through him,
with him,
in him,
in the unity of the Holy Spirit,
all glory and honour is yours,
almighty Father,
for ever and ever.

P. **Amen.**

Rite Of Communion

C. Let us pray with confidence to the Father
in the words our Saviour gave us:

All. **Our Father, who art in heaven,**
hallowed be thy name;
Thy kingdom come;
Thy will be done on earth as it is in heaven.
Give us this day our daily bread;
and forgive us our trespasses
as we forgive those who trespass against us;
and lead us not into temptation,
but deliver us from evil.

C. Deliver us, Lord, from every evil,
and grant us peace in our day.
In your mercy keep us free from sin
and protect us from all anxiety
as we wait in joyful hope
for the coming of our Saviour, Jesus Christ.

All. **For the kingdom, the power, and the glory are yours,**
now and for ever.

C. Lord Jesus Christ, you said to your apostles:
I leave you peace, my peace I give you.
Look not on our sins, but on the faith of your Church,
and grant us the peace and unity of your kingdom
where you live for ever and ever.

P. **Amen.**

C. The peace of the Lord be with you always.

P. **And also with you.**

[*Then the deacon, or the priest, may add:*

C. Let us offer each other the sign of peace.

All make a sign of peace according to local custom.]

C. May this mingling of the body and blood of our Lord Jesus Christ
bring eternal life to us who receive it.

Meanwhile the following is sung or said:

All. **Lamb of God, you take away the sins of the world:**
have mercy on us.
Lamb of God, you take away the sins of the world:
have mercy on us.
Lamb of God, you take away the sins of the world:
grant us peace.

C. Lord Jesus Christ, Son of the living God,
by the will of the Father and the work of the Holy Spirit
your death brought life to the world.
By your holy body and blood
free me from all my sins and from every evil.
Keep me faithful to your teaching,
and never let me be parted from you.

or

Lord Jesus Christ,
with faith in your love and mercy

I eat your body and drink your blood.
Let it not bring me condemnation,
but health in mind and body.

C. This is the Lamb of God
who takes away the sins of the world.
Happy are those who are called to his supper.
All. **Lord, I am not worthy to receive you,
but only say the word and I shall be healed.**

The priest's communion

While the priest is receiving the body of Christ, the communion song is begun.

The people's communion

C. The body of Christ.
P. **Amen.**

After the communion of the people, a period of silence may be observed, or a psalm or song of praise may be sung. Then:

C. Let us pray.

Priest and people pray in silence for a while, unless the silence has already been observed. Then the priest sings or says the prayer after communion. The people respond:

P. **Amen.**

Concluding rite

If there are any short announcements, they are made at this time. Then:

C. The Lord be with you.
P. **And also with you.**
C. May almighty God bless you, the Father, and the Son, and the Holy Spirit.
P. **Amen.**
C. The Mass is ended, go in peace.
P. **Thanks be to God.**

Alternative dismissals

C. Go in the peace of Christ.
or
C. Go in peace to love and serve the Lord.
P. **Thanks be to God.**

INDEX

MORNING PRAYERS

NIGHT PRAYERS

PRAYERS FOR CONFESSION

INDEX

ROSARY THOUGHTS

PRAYERS OF ST AUGUSTINE

PRAYERS OF CARDINAL NEWMAN

INDEX

PRAYERS OF ARCHBISHOP GOODIER

PRAYERS OF ADORATION, CONFIDENCE AND OFFERING

PRAYERS TO OUR LORD AND HIS SACRED HEART

INDEX

PRAYERS FOR ONESELF

PRAYERS BEFORE COMMUNION

PRAYERS AFTER COMMUNION